הגדה של פסח

Freedom of the Soul

HAGGADAH

הגדה של פסח

Freedom of the Soul

HAGGADAH

Rabbi Dovid Goldwasser

ISBN 1-880582-8-64

The Judaica Press, Inc.
718-972-6200 800-972-6201
info@judaicapress.com
visit us on the web at: www.judaicapress.com

Manufactured in the United States of America

מכתב
מאת הגאון הצדיק פאר דורינו,
מרן רבי אביגדור מיללער זצללה"ה

ב"ה

כבר נתפרסם הרב דוד גאלדוואסער במעשיו הרבים כאיש הרוח מדריך בני אדם בדרך התורה, ועכשיו מוסיף גם בחיבורו זה ללכת בדרכו לעורר ולעודד ולפחת נשמת חיים בקרב רבים מבני עמנו. יצליחוהו ה' בכל מעשיו ויפוצו דברי השפעתו בישראל.

נאום

אביגדור הכהן מיללער

אביגדור הכהן מיללער

מכתב ברכה ועידוד זה קיבל הרה"ג המחבר שליט"א ממרן הגה"צ **רבי אביגדור הכהן מיללער** זצללה"ה זמן קצר טרם הסתלקותו לחיי עוה"ב, והוא א' ממכתביו האחרונים שכתב בעצמו, ברוב חביבותו למורינו המחבר שליט"א, לכן אמרנו להדפיס המכתב כאן.

♦ ♦ ♦ *Dedication* ♦ ♦ ♦

With love and admiration, we dedicate this Haggadah to our dear grandparents, parents and family.

♦ ♦ ♦

To Our Grandparents

Yosef Eliyahu and Ettel Koenig ז״ל

Yosef Yehoshua and Malka Orenstein ז״ל

Rose and Shloime Zalmen Klein ז״ל

(Klein Basći)

Margit and Leopold Mandl ז״ל

♦ ♦ ♦

To Our Parents

Chaim Shlome and Chaya Yitte Koenig נ״י

Mordechai Yitzchok "Béla" Klein ז״ל

Rochel Malka "Zsuszsi" Mandl נ״י

♦ ♦ ♦ *Dedication* ♦ ♦ ♦

To Our Family

Ettie and Gershon Yona Kaufman
Yossi and Pearl Koenig
Moishe and Sheindy Koenig
Yankie and Mindy Koenig
Shmuel Nuta and Ora Koenig
Avrumy and Feige Greenblatt
Mechie and Minna Koenig
Estie and Avrom Cohen
Chaim and Shaindy Rabinowitz
Shaye Binyomin and Rachel (Ruchel) Brull
Avrumy and Kathy Jordan
Alexander (Sendy) and Mindy Goodman
Judy Klein
and all of our nieces, nephews, and cousins

♦ ♦ ♦

To Our Dear Children

Miriam Bayla and Devorah (Devoiry) Klein

♦ ♦ ♦

In recognition of the dedication, love, and warmth that we have shared throughout the years, and especially on Pesach nights, we express our gratitude by dedicating this Haggadah to our dear family.

It is our tefillah that we and our children emulate your incredible goodness and preserve this blessed and sacred legacy.

♦ ♦ ♦

Gittie and Gary (מאיר יהודה) Klein

Acknowledgements

In appreciation of Maran HaGaon HaRav Simcha Wasserman zt"l, whose awe-inspiring life is forever with me, and Maran HaGaon HaRav Avigdor Miller zt"l, whose *hashpo'oh* is felt wherever Jews are found. Their inspiration and encouragement will forever be present.

To Martin E. Friedlander, Esq., a unique leader whose vision for the future has guided countless individuals and organizations בדרך התורה. His *mesiras nefesh* and keen interest in every aspect of this sefer is responsible for its publication. It is my privilege to have his partnership in so many worthwhile undertakings. May Hashem grant him, his wife Liba, and their exceptional children, Yehudis, Moshe Dovid, Shimmy, and Yitzchok continued blessing, success and simchas.

To Gary and Gittie Klein, who have dedicated this book, and whose enthusiasm and encouragement have brought many projects to fruition. Gary and Gittie are exemplary role models of Torah *askonim* for all to emulate. They continue their family's golden chain of tradition of mitzvos and *maasim tovim*. Their warmth, wisdom and understanding have impacted on our community and changed it for the better. I thank Hashem for our special *kesher*. May their outstanding children, Miriam and Devory, be a source of continued nachas for the entire *mishpocho*.

To Reb Chaim and Barbara Kamenetsky, whose *ahavas Yisroel* knows no bounds. Their legendary work on behalf of Klal Yisroel serves as an inspiration to people everywhere from all walks of life. I cherish the *ahavas achim* that exists between us. This sefer has been dedicated *l'iluy nishmas* Reb Chaim's mother, מרת שיינא טובה בת בנימין ע"ה. Mrs. Kamenetsky was an unusual melumedes, an eishes chayil of regal bearing. She personified the posuk, *"V'soras chesed al l'shonah."* I was *zoche* to see her on *Acharon shel Pesach,* the last day of her life, as she participated in the divrei Torah and the *niggunim* that were being sung in the dining room. I will never forget the visible simchas yom tov that she had being together with her *choshuve* family and acheinu Bnei Yisroel. She left an indelible impression upon all who were privileged to know her.

To Howie and Rachelle Sirota, Esqs. who staunchly support and encourage every project. It is a personal privilege for me to be so closely associated with outstanding people whose lives are dedicated to helping others. May they, together with their beloved parents, Simon and Harriet

Rofé, reap the rich rewards of their efforts and be blessed spiritually and materially.

To R' Aryeh Mezei of Judaica Press for all of his efforts on behalf of the Klal. His creative and perceptive insights have truly enhanced the field of Jewish publishing. His sincerity and enthusiasm for his *avodas hakodesh* inspires people the world over. May he have continued *brocho v'hatzlocho* in all his magnificent efforts *l'hagdil Torah ul'haadirah*. Thanks also to the Judaica Press team who helped edit this sefer, including Bonnie Goldman, Zisi Berkowitz and Chana Leah Hirschhorn. Special thanks to Nachum Shapiro of Judaica Press, whose expertise and professionalism have also contributed to the making of this book.

To the *mispallelim* of Khal Bais Yitzchok of Flatbush, for their inspiration, and the privilege of being the Rov of such a *choshuve kehillah*.

To the following people for their support and assistance in this project: Rabbi Moshe Kolodny, Rabbi Simcha Kornreich, Eliezer and Gitti Allman, Eliezer and Helen Appelbaum, Heshy and Aliza Barth, Chazzan Ira and Alyssa Heller, Dror and Susan Kahn, Leib and Linda Koyfman, Jonathan and Yehudis Lewis, Rabbi and Mrs. Zechariah Lomnitz, Shaindy Mendelsohn, Rabbi Duvie and Feigie Neuhauser, Mrs. Sonjia Samokovlija. There are additional names of *tayere chaverim* too numerous to list—*chaverim kol Yisroel*.

To Mrs. Simi Eichorn for her untiring efforts on behalf of this book, seeing the manuscript through from its earliest stages. Her valuable suggestions and considerable knowledge have enhanced the pages of this book. May she and her choshuve mishpocho go from simcha to simcha לאוי"ט.

To Mrs. F. Blum for a masterful job in helping to edit the English manuscript. Her insight and talent have enabled me to precisely capture the essence of this sefer.

To Nachum Segal, renowned radio personality, a master of words and an eloquent spokesman for Klal Yisroel. It is a privilege to work together with R' Nachum for close to two decades. His unique talents and *kochos* have united people from all walks of life.

To editor Steve Walz for his wisdom, constant support, and encouragement. He is a powerful advocate for truth, justice, and unity. We are blessed that he shares his considerable talents with the international community.

Forever etched in my *neshomoh* is the *mesiras nefesh* of my beloved parents, *avi mori* R' Yitzchok ben R' Yeruchom and *immi morasi* Riva

Tzirna bas R' Benzion ז"ל. May the example of their noble lives always serve as a source of inspiration and blessing.

To my dear in-laws, Mr. and Mrs. Ben and Esther Koval, who carry on the royal lineage of the distinguished Kovalenko and Fink families. May they merit much *nachas* from their children, *einiklach* and *ur-einiklach*.

ברכה והצלחה אריכות ימים ושנות טובות

To my eishes chayil, Hinda Chaya, לאוי"ט. נתן הקב"ה בינה יתירה באשה—To be sure none of my work on behalf of the *klal* would be possible without her *mesiras nefesh*. May we merit much *nachas* from our dear children, Rabbi Chesky, Fayge and Yitzchok Holtzberg; Yeruchum and Gittel Goldwasser; Eliyahu; and Dassy. May they always go בדרך שהנחיל לנו אבותינו הקדושים, and may we merit to see בנים ובני בנים עוסקים בתורה ובמצוות לעולמי עד.

Brooklyn, New York
Hametzapeh L'yeshua
Rabbi Dovid Goldwasser

Introduction

"והלחת מעשה אלוקים המה והמכתב מכתב אלוקים
הוא חרות על הלחת—אל תקרא חרות אלא חרות שאין
לך בן חורין אלא מי שעוסק בתלמוד תורה" (אבות ו:ב)

The luchos were Hashem's work, and the writing was Hashem's writing, חרות—engraved—on the luchos.

Do not read חָרוּת, engraved, but חֵרוּת, freedom, for no one is free except one who is occupied with Torah study.

Although in its proper context, חרות means engraved, Chazal tell us that it can also be read חרות meaning freedom. However, the posuk's simple meaning does not change. The new interpretation simply provides us with an additional meaning, one that complements the first, reinforcing both the meaning and the message.

The letters on the luchos were engraved, rather than written, because writing is impermanent. Writing can be erased, faded, or painted over. But little can obliterate the chiseled word. The engraved letters of the luchos were an inseparable part of the stone. They were not a separate entity; they were the luchos.

To enjoy the freedom of Torah study, we must first engrave the Torah's words onto our hearts. The Torah is not simply a cold acquisition of knowledge; it is deeper than that, it must become a part of us, profoundly engraved onto our being. Its indelible impression will free our souls from limitations and from worldly restrictions.

The freedom of a Torah life results directly from the letters of the luchos being engraved onto our hearts. The two definitions of חרות are thus intertwined.

♦ ♦ ♦ ♦ ♦ ♦

In 1981 I visited the former Soviet Union, home to hundreds of thousands of Jews robbed of their heritage. Those were the days before Communism's fall; the days when Jews were forbidden to observe their religion. They were the days of the refuseniks, which is what the men and women who were refused exit visas were known as.

I was in the Soviet Union on a mission. My task was to offer chizuk to our oppressed brethren, to encourage them, and answer their questions. But it was I who was strengthened by them, particularly by one refusenik named Ari.

Ari was being monitored by the KGB, the internal security agency and intelligence office of the then-Soviet Union. He had earned this distinction by applying for a visa to leave the country. Once it was discovered that he had applied for a visa, he lost his job and basic civil liberties. Still, he persevered; even after he had been refused permission, he still repeatedly applied for a visa in the hope that he would one day realize his dream of living in freedom.

On the night we met with Ari, the frigid Russian winter whipped us with its fury. We could not drive directly to his home; we dared not risk detection. It was dangerous in those days for any one in the Soviet Union to meet with foreigners, particularly while they were being monitored by the KGB. In fact, Ari would not even give us his address. Instead, he arranged for a friend to meet us on a deserted corner, and direct us to his apartment.

We were struck by the poverty in Ari's house. But Ari had devoted his life to Torah. He spent the evening discussing his Torah studies with me, and asking halachic questions. It was Torah *lishmoh* at its finest. Only toward the end of our visit did Ari mention anything about his personal situation. He spoke quietly about his experience of persecution, poverty, and pain. It was heartbreaking to hear. Finally, my colleague could bear it no longer.

"We can't wait for you to be free!" he cried. Ari looked at him with utter tranquility.

"I already am free," he said, "for no one is free except one who is occupied with Torah study."

May we soon hear the footsteps of Moshiach Tzidkeinu, who will usher in a new era of freedom of the soul.

הגדה של פסח

פירוש

רב דוד גאלדוואסער

The Seder Plate

The following items are arranged on the Seder plate.

1. ***Zeroa***—a roasted shankbone;
2. ***Beitzah***—a hard-boiled egg;
3. ***Marror***—bitter herbs (commonly either horseradish or romaine lettuce);
4. ***Charoses***—a mixture of wine, chopped nuts, apples, and cinnamon;
5. ***Karpas***—a green vegetable (such as celery, parsley, lettuce, cucumbers or potatoes).

Measurements

According to Rabbi Dovid Feinstein, shlit"a, the following proportions of wine, matzah and other foods must be eaten during the Seder ceremony—with the exception of the meal itself.

1. ***Wine***—3.3 fluid ounces of wine for each of the four cups of wine must be drunk. If the Seder is held on Friday night, 4.42 fluid ounces of wine for each cup should be drunk.
2. ***Matzah***—after the blessing over the matzah is said, a minimum of 7 inches by 6.25 inches piece of matzah is required to be eaten.
3. ***Korech***—a piece of matzah and marror sandwich equal to at least 7 inches by 4 inches must be eaten.
4. ***Marror***—if grated horseradish is used, 1 fluid ounce must be eaten. If romaine lettuce leaves are used, then the required amount should cover an area equal to 8 by 10 inches.

בְּדִיקַת חָמֵץ

On the evening before the Pesach Seder we conduct the search for leaven, "bedikas chametz." (If Pesach begins on Saturday evening, the search is conducted the previous Thursday evening.) The search is done by candlelight. Customarily, ten small pieces of bread are placed around the house before the search so that leaven will be found during the search.

Before beginning the search, we light a candle and recite the following blessing:

בָּרוּךְ אַתָּה יְיָ אֱלֹהֵינוּ מֶלֶךְ הָעוֹלָם, אֲשֶׁר קִדְּשָׁנוּ בְּמִצְוֹתָיו, וְצִוָּנוּ עַל בִּעוּר חָמֵץ.

Every room of the house is searched with a lit candle. After the search has been conducted and the remaining leaven has been wrapped up, the following statement is recited:

כָּל חֲמִירָא וַחֲמִיעָה דְּאִכָּא בִרְשׁוּתִי דְּלָא חֲמִתֵּהּ וּדְלָא בִעַרְתֵּהּ וּדְלָא יְדַעְנָא לֵהּ לִבָּטֵל וְלֶהֱוֵי הֶפְקֵר כְּעַפְרָא דְאַרְעָא.

◆ פירוש ◆

בְּדִיקַת חָמֵץ

Weeks before Yom Tov we begin to rid our homes of chametz. By the night of the 13th of Nissan, the only chametz we should have is the food we plan to eat in the morning. On the night of bedikas chametz, we perform the search for chametz, searching our homes for any trace of leaven that may have remained. As part of the procedure, *kol chamirah* is recited. We declare:

כָּל חֲמִירָא וַחֲמִיעָה דְּאִכָּא בִרְשׁוּתִי דְּלָא חֲמִתֵּהּ וּדְלָא בִעַרְתֵּהּ
וּדְלָא יְדַעְנָא לֵהּ לִבָּטֵל וְלֶהֱוֵי הֶפְקֵר כְּעַפְרָא דְאַרְעָא.

"Any type of leaven that may still be in my possession, that I have not seen or not removed, or that I do not know about, let it be considered nullified and ownerless, like the dust of the earth."

The famous 19th century tzaddik, R' Boruch of Mezhibozh, would say

Bedikas Chametz

On the evening before the Pesach Seder we conduct the search for leaven, "bedikas chametz." (If Pesach begins on Saturday evening, the search is conducted the previous Thursday evening.) The search is done by candlelight. Customarily, ten small pieces of bread are placed around the house before the search so that leaven will be found during the search.

Before beginning the search, we light a candle and recite the following blessing:

Blessed are you, Hashem our God, King of the universe, Who has sanctified us with His commandments, and commanded us concerning the removal of leaven.

Every room of the house is searched with a lit candle. After the search has been conducted and the remaining leaven has been wrapped up, the following statement is recited:

Any type of leaven that may still be in my possession, that I have not seen or not removed, or that I do not know about, let it be considered nullified and ownerless, like the dust of the earth.

◆ פירוש ◆

that "any leaven that may still be in my possession" refers to egotistic negative traits. In general, the leaven that we clean from our homes before Pesach represents the negative traits that we should simultaneously be "cleaning" from ourselves.

R' Boruch declared: "These poor middos that may be part of me, both those that I am aware of and those that I am not aware of, should be considered null and void. I ask Hashem for His help in ridding myself of these undesirable traits, and removing them completely from my life." When we say כָּל חֲמִירָא we should similarly ask Hashem to help us rid ourselves of any bad middos.

It's not easy, however, to purge ourselves of bad middos. It takes hard work and dedication, something that we have to be willing to commit to. This was illustrated by Rav Zalman Yudkin, the well-known *menahel* of Kiryat Malachi in Eretz Yisroel. Once, while we were talking, Rav Yudkin noticed that one of the seforim on the bookshelf was turned

בִּעוּר חָמֵץ

On the morning following bedikas chametz (if Pesach begins on Saturday evening, then this is done on Friday morning), all of the remaining leaven in the house is burned, including the leaven found on the search of the previous night.

The following statement is then recited:

כָּל חֲמִירָא וַחֲמִיעָה דְּאִכָּא בִרְשׁוּתִי דַּחֲזִתֵּהּ וּדְלָא חֲזִתֵּהּ, דַּחֲמִתֵּהּ וּדְלָא חֲמִתֵּהּ, דְּבִעַרְתֵּהּ וּדְלָא בִעַרְתֵּהּ, לִבָּטֵל וְלֶהֱוֵי הֶפְקֵר כְּעַפְרָא דְאַרְעָא.

♦ פירוש ♦

upside down. The Rav rose, turned the sefer right side up, and returned it to the shelf.

"Perhaps you could straighten me out, too?" someone in the room asked.

Rav Yudkin smiled, and, with a twinkle in his eye answered, "That you'll have to do for yourself."

♦ ♦ ♦ ♦ ♦ ♦

Thus as we clean our homes for Pesach, it is clear that we must keep in mind that not only our physical homes must be cleaned; our entire being has to be prepared. And while it is proper to pray for assistance, our spiritual cleansing still requires vigorous and focused work on our part.

R' Yisroel Yaakov Lubchansky, who was the mashgiach of the great Baranovich yeshiva, asks: Why are we so exacting in cleaning our home and distancing ourselves from chametz? Why isn't any other forbidden food treated with such severity?

He explains that chametz is considered to represent the yetzer hora, and the Torah tells us that strictness is required to rid oneself of the yetzer hora's influence. It is not enough to simply refrain from eating chametz. Aggressive action is necessary so that no trace of the evil should remain within us.

Burning the Chametz

On the morning following bedikas chametz (if Pesach begins on Saturday evening, then this is done on Friday morning), all of the remaining leaven in the house is burned, including the leaven found on the search of the previous night.

The following statement is then recited:

Any type of leaven that may still be in my possession, that I may or may not have seen, found or removed, let it be considered nullified and ownerless, like the dust of the earth.

♦ פירוש ♦

The following story powerfully illustrates why being stringent with oneself regarding the yetzer hora is important.

A middle-aged man once came to his rebbe and told him that he had a store which he had inherited from his father, and that though he conducted the business identically to his father, business had declined and there were almost no customers left.

The rebbe asked him, "What did your father do when there were no customers in the store?" The son thought about it for a minute and answered, "Why, he would open a Gemarah and learn."

The rebbe smiled, "And what do *you* do when there are no customers in the store?"

The son shrugged and replied, "*Nu*, what should I tell you, rebbe? I read the newspaper or I just sit around."

"If this is the case," the rebbe explained, "it is quite clear. The yetzer hora sent customers to your father in order to interrupt him from his Torah learning. However, the yetzer hora doesn't have the same incentive in your situation."

♦ ♦ ♦ ♦ ♦ ♦

When Hashem spoke to Moshe, He asked him to tell the Jewish nation, "אני ה', והוצאתי אתכם . . . וגאלתי אתכם . . . בזרוע נטוי"—I am Hashem,

עֵרוּב תַּבְשִׁילִין

When the first day of Pesach falls on a Thursday, in order to be able to cook on Friday for Shabbos, one must prepare an Eruv Tavshilin *on the Wednesday afternoon before Yom Tov begins.*

One takes a piece of matzah and any cooked food—such as a piece of meat or fish, or a cooked egg—places them on a plate, raises it, and recites the following blessing and statement:

בָּרוּךְ אַתָּה יְיָ אֱלֹהֵינוּ מֶלֶךְ הָעוֹלָם, אֲשֶׁר קִדְּשָׁנוּ בְּמִצְוֹתָיו, וְצִוָּנוּ עַל מִצְוַת עֵרוּב.

בַּהֲדֵין עֵרוּבָא יְהֵא שָׁרֵא לָנָא לַאֲפוּיֵי וּלְבַשּׁוּלֵי וּלְאַטְמוּנֵי וּלְאַדְלוּקֵי שְׁרָגָא וּלְתַקָּנָא וּלְמֶעְבַּד כָּל צָרְכָנָא, מִיּוֹמָא טָבָא לְשַׁבַּתָּא [לָנוּ וּלְכָל יִשְׂרָאֵל הַדָּרִים בָּעִיר הַזֹּאת].

♦ פירוש ♦

and I will take you out of Egypt… and I will liberate you…with an outstretched arm."

HaGaon HaRav Avigdor Miller zt"l asked: Why was *yetzias* Mitzrayim, and all of the miracles surrounding it, necessary? It would have been quite natural for the Egyptians to decide to expel the Jews on their own. The Torah even tells us that when the Jews were multiplying at such an alarming rate, Pharaoh convened his advisors to decide what to do about the Jews. "הבה נתחכמה לו—Let us deal with this wisely," he said.

Wouldn't it have been wise for Pharaoh to expel such a people—if they presented such a risk to the Egyptians? Why didn't Hashem simply cause Pharaoh to expel the Jews, which would have eliminated the need for a miraculous deliverance?

The answer is that *yetzias* Mitzrayim entailed much more then the redemption of the Jews. It revealed Hashem's greatness.

Hashem told Moshe that Egypt would know, "that I am Hashem." This

Eruv Tavshilin

When the first day of Pesach falls on a Thursday, in order to be able to cook on Friday for Shabbos, one must prepare an Eruv Tavshilin *on the Wednesday afternoon before Yom Tov begins.*

One takes a piece of matzah and any cooked food—such as a piece of meat or fish, or a cooked egg—places them on a plate, raises it, and recites the following blessing and statement:

Blessed are you, Hashem our God, King of the universe, Who has sanctified us with His commandments, and commanded us concerning the commandment of the *eruv*.

With this *eruv*, let it be permitted for us to bake, cook, and keep food warm, to light candles, to tend to and take care of all our needs, from Yom Tov to Shabbos (for us, and for all Jews that dwell in this city).

♦ פירוש ♦

revelation of Hashem's existence, the Absolute God, was an integral part of the redemption of the Jews. This is why the miracles were necessary.

The plagues, the redemption, and *kriyas Yam Suf* all manifested Hashem's outstretched arm, and also led the Jewish People to recognize Hashem's presence and His strength. When the Jews cried to Hashem, they each became personally aware that He, and only He, could spare them. As the *makkos* progressed, this realization grew, and it peaked when they witnessed the splitting of the *Yam Suf*.

Nevertheless, Hashem's "outstretched arm" was not reserved only for that era. Rather, it is a pact for all generations. In *Maseches Chagigah* (5:2) the Gemarah tells of an *apikores* who visited Rabbi Yehoshua.

"Your God has abandoned you!" the *apikores* exclaimed. "He has turned His face away from you!"

Rabbi Yehoshua lifted his arm, and said, "Hashem's arm is still outstretched over us, as it was in Mitzrayim."

The miracles in Mitzrayim exist for eternity. They loudly proclaim to the world that Hashem is the One Who performs miracles—both openly

סימני הסדר

קַדֵּשׁ	מָרוֹר.
וּרְחַץ.	כּוֹרֵךְ.
כַּרְפַּס.	שֻׁלְחָן עוֹרֵךְ.
יַחַץ.	צָפוּן.
מַגִּיד.	בָּרֵךְ.
רָחְצָה.	הַלֵּל.
מוֹצִיא. מַצָּה.	נִרְצָה.

♦ פ י ר ו ש ♦

and under nature's guise. Even when we do not witness open miracles, we can be assured that His "outstretched arm" still protects us, and that His love for us will last forever.

People who immerse themselves in Torah and mitzvos are aware of this outstretched arm each moment of each day. In today's times, we need not look far. Those who look for the זרוע נטויה (outstretched arm) will see it clearly, at every step of their lives.

♦ ♦ ♦ ♦ ♦ ♦

קַדֵּשׁ וּרְחַץ...

We now enumerate the fifteen *simanei haseder* (parts of the Seder) before we begin with Kiddush.

Why do we recite the Seder's order before we begin? Wouldn't the order become evident as the Seder progresses?

One reason this is done is to demonstrate the importance of order. Our Rabbis have stressed that we should always know how and when to do things, and that all our plans should be considered through the proper perspective. With respect to every action that we take, we must always ask, "Is this what the Torah wants me to do?"

Simanei HaSeder

Kadesh	Recite kiddush
Urechatz	Wash hands
Karpas	Eat vegetable dipped in salt water
Yachatz	Break the middle matzah
Maggid	Recite the Hagaddah
Rochtzah	Wash one's hands (before eating matzah)
Motzi	Recite "Hamotzi," on the matzos
Matzah	Recite "Al achilas matzah," and eat the matzah
Marror	Eat the bitter herbs dipped in charoset
Korech	Eat the matzah and marror sandwich
Shulchan Orech	Eat the meal
Tzafun	Eat the Afikomen
Borech	Recite Birkas Hamazon
Hallel	Recite Hallel
Nirtzah	Our Seder service is accepted and concluded

♦ פירוש ♦

To illustrate, when the Vizhnitzer Rebbe, author of the classic Torah commentary, *Imrei Chaim,* first arrived in Eretz Yisroel, for example, he asked someone, "How are you?"

The man answered, *"hakol beseder"* (everything is in order).

The Rebbe enjoyed the response. "You don't even know how right you are!" he replied, "because *hakol b'*seder—everything revolves around the Pesach Seder. Everything is dependent on what happens at the Seder."

What the Rebbe meant was that the various actions we partake in during the Seder are a *siman* for things that will occur in our lives during the year. From the Seder we derive encouragement and sustenance.

So the Seder is begun with a list of the actions we will be performing. It's our agenda. It helps us prepare for the evening, set our goals, and put ourselves in the appropriate frame of mind to follow through.

קַדֵּשׁ

When the Pesach Seder occurs on Friday evening, begin here.
On other nights begin on page 28.

(וַיְהִי עֶרֶב וַיְהִי בֹקֶר יוֹם הַשִּׁשִּׁי, וַיְכֻלּוּ הַשָּׁמַיִם וְהָאָרֶץ וְכָל צְבָאָם: וַיְכַל אֱלֹהִים בַּיּוֹם הַשְּׁבִיעִי, מְלַאכְתּוֹ אֲשֶׁר עָשָׂה, וַיִּשְׁבֹּת בַּיּוֹם הַשְּׁבִיעִי, מִכָּל מְלַאכְתּוֹ אֲשֶׁר עָשָׂה: וַיְבָרֶךְ אֱלֹהִים אֶת יוֹם הַשְּׁבִיעִי, וַיְקַדֵּשׁ אֹתוֹ, כִּי בוֹ שָׁבַת מִכָּל מְלַאכְתּוֹ, אֲשֶׁר בָּרָא אֱלֹהִים לַעֲשׂוֹת:)

♦ פ י ר ו ש ♦

Another reason the order of the Seder is recited before we actually begin the Seder is because we should always prepare in advance (הכנות) for mitzvos. Both thought and preparation are required before we approach holiness.

Our lives are not lived haphazardly; rather, every important thing we do requires proper preparation so that we can accomplish all that is necessary.

Chazal say, "מי שטרח בערב שבת יאכל בשבת—one who busies oneself and prepares on Erev Shabbos will have food to eat on Shabbos." Homiletically, Erev Shabbos is compared to our existence in this world, whereas Shabbos is our life in Olam Habah (the next world). People who prepare themselves in this world through a life of Torah and mitzvos will enjoy the fruits of their labor as their portion in Olam Habah.

One man who spent his Erev Shabbos (his life) preparing for "Shabbos" (Olam Haba) was HaRav Avigdor Miller zt"l. Rav Miller was once asked why he would not be attending a certain public event. Rav Miller explained that he had to prepare for the test. The questioner looked puzzled. What test was Rav Miller talking about? Rav Miller explained that after 120 years we stand before the Heavenly Court, when the ultimate test will have to be passed.

Kadesh

When the Pesach Seder occurs on Friday evening, begin here.
On other nights begin on page 29.

It was evening and it was morning on the sixth day. And the heavens and the earth were completed and all their hosts. And God completed on the seventh day all the work that He had done, and He abstained on the seventh day from all the work that He had done. And God blessed the seventh day and sanctified it, for thereon He abstained from all His work that God had created to do.

קַדֵּשׁ
כִּי בָנוּ בָחַרְתָּ

"What is so special about the Jewish people that we say that Hashem chose us?" asks the Baal HaTanya, Rabbi Schneur Zalman of Liadi.

He explains that our uniqueness is more than just spiritual. It is physical as well. Hashem gave us many practical mitzvos in order that we would make use of all of the many different aspects of the physical world to achieve closeness with Hashem. This particular spiritual path is something unique to the Jews.

♦ ♦ ♦ ♦ ♦ ♦

One person who elevated the physical to a spiritual level was the world renowned Sephardic gaon, Rabbi Yisrael Abuchatzeirah, known as Baba Sali. He was famous for his miraculous power of sight. When someone asked him how he was able to see the unseeable, he replied: "I use my eyes, just like any other person. But I make certain that my eyes see only what they should, and I never look at anything forbidden."

An explanation of this can be found in the words of the Alter of Slabodka. The Alter says that Hashem created every person with the ability to see from one end of the world to the other. It is only nature that

When the Pesach Seder occurs on a weekday, begin here:

סַבְרִי מָרָנָן וְרַבָּנָן וְרַבּוֹתַי:

בָּרוּךְ אַתָּה יְיָ, אֱלֹהֵינוּ מֶלֶךְ הָעוֹלָם, בּוֹרֵא פְּרִי הַגָּפֶן:

בָּרוּךְ אַתָּה יְיָ, אֱלֹהֵינוּ מֶלֶךְ הָעוֹלָם, אֲשֶׁר בָּחַר בָּנוּ מִכָּל עָם, וְרוֹמְמָנוּ מִכָּל לָשׁוֹן, וְקִדְּשָׁנוּ בְּמִצְוֹתָיו, וַתִּתֶּן לָנוּ יְיָ אֱלֹהֵינוּ בְּאַהֲבָה (לשבת שַׁבָּתוֹת לִמְנוּחָה וּ)מוֹעֲדִים לְשִׂמְחָה, חַגִּים וּזְמַנִּים לְשָׂשׂוֹן אֶת יוֹם (לשבת הַשַּׁבָּת הַזֶּה וְאֶת יוֹם) חַג הַמַּצּוֹת הַזֶּה. זְמַן חֵרוּתֵנוּ, (לשבת בְּאַהֲבָה) מִקְרָא קֹדֶשׁ, זֵכֶר לִיצִיאַת מִצְרָיִם. כִּי בָנוּ בָחַרְתָּ וְאוֹתָנוּ קִדַּשְׁתָּ מִכָּל הָעַמִּים. (לשבת וְשַׁבָּת) וּמוֹעֲדֵי קָדְשֶׁךָ (לשבת בְּאַהֲבָה וּבְרָצוֹן) בְּשִׂמְחָה וּבְשָׂשׂוֹן הִנְחַלְתָּנוּ: בָּרוּךְ אַתָּה יְיָ, מְקַדֵּשׁ (לשבת הַשַּׁבָּת וְ)יִשְׂרָאֵל וְהַזְּמַנִּים:

On Saturday evening, add the following two blessings. On all other nights, skip to the blessing, Shehecheyanu, *below:*

Look towards the Yom Tov candles as this blessing is recited:

(**בָּרוּךְ** אַתָּה יְיָ, אֱלֹהֵינוּ מֶלֶךְ הָעוֹלָם, בּוֹרֵא מְאוֹרֵי הָאֵשׁ:

בָּרוּךְ אַתָּה יְיָ, אֱלֹהֵינוּ מֶלֶךְ הָעוֹלָם, הַמַּבְדִּיל בֵּין קֹדֶשׁ לְחֹל בֵּין אוֹר לְחֹשֶׁךְ, בֵּין יִשְׂרָאֵל לָעַמִּים, בֵּין יוֹם הַשְּׁבִיעִי לְשֵׁשֶׁת יְמֵי הַמַּעֲשֶׂה. בֵּין קְדֻשַּׁת שַׁבָּת לִקְדֻשַּׁת יוֹם טוֹב הִבְדַּלְתָּ. וְאֶת יוֹם הַשְּׁבִיעִי מִשֵּׁשֶׁת יְמֵי הַמַּעֲשֶׂה קִדַּשְׁתָּ. הִבְדַּלְתָּ וְקִדַּשְׁתָּ אֶת עַמְּךָ יִשְׂרָאֵל בִּקְדֻשָּׁתֶךָ. בָּרוּךְ אַתָּה יְיָ, הַמַּבְדִּיל בֵּין קֹדֶשׁ לְקֹדֶשׁ:)

בָּרוּךְ אַתָּה יְיָ, אֱלֹהֵינוּ מֶלֶךְ הָעוֹלָם, שֶׁהֶחֱיָנוּ וְקִיְּמָנוּ וְהִגִּיעָנוּ לַזְּמַן הַזֶּה:

Drink the first cup of wine while reclining on the left side.

When the Pesach Seder occurs on a weekday, begin here:

Attention our masters and our teachers:

Blessed are You, Hashem, our God, King of the universe, Who creates the fruit of the vine.

Blessed are You, Hashem, our God, King of the universe, Who has chosen us from every nation, exalted us above every language, and sanctified us with His commandments. You have given us, Hashem, our God, with love, (*on Friday evening add:* Sabbaths for rest, and) festivals for happiness, holidays and seasons for joy, this day of (*on Friday evening add:* Shabbos and this day of) the holiday of matzos, the season of our freedom, (*on Friday evening add:* with love) a holy assembly, commemorating the Exodus from Egypt. For You have chosen us, and You have sanctified us above all the nations, and Your (*on Friday evening add:* Shabbos and) holy festivals (*on Friday evening add:* with love and favor) in happiness and joy You granted us. Blessed are you, Hashem, Who sanctifies (*on Friday evening add:* Shabbos,) Israel, and the seasons.

On Saturday evening, add the following two blessings. On all other nights, skip to the blessing, Shehecheyanu, *Who has kept us alive, below:*

Look towards the Yom Tov candles as this blessing is recited:

Blessed are You, Hashem, our God, King of the universe, Who creates the lights of fire.

Blessed are you, Hashem, our God, King of the universe, Who separates between holy and ordinary, between light and darkness, between Israel and the nations, and between the seventh day and the six work days. Between the sanctity of Shabbos and the sanctity of a Yom Tov You divided, and the seventh day from the six work days You sanctified. You have separated and sanctified Your people Israel with Your own holiness. Blessed are you, Hashem, Who divided between holy and holy.

Blessed are you, Hashem, our God, King of the universe, Who has kept us alive, preserved us, and enabled us to reach this season.

Drink the first cup of wine while reclining on the left side.

We wash our hands, but do not recite the customary blessing.

impedes our view. But people who control their nature can see what they were created to see.

Similarly, Rebbe Nachman of Breslov says that if we feel a weakness in one of our limbs, we should strengthen the spiritual power of that part of our body. For instance, if our voice weakens, we should make sure to speak only what is permitted. We should steer clear of forbidden speech such as lashon hara. To further strengthen our voice we should use speech for spiritual purposes like Torah study, prayer, and encouraging those in need.

♦ ♦ ♦ ♦ ♦ ♦

Why do we first sanctify ourselves with קדש and only afterwards purify ourselves with ורחץ? It is written in Tehillim (34:15), "סור מרע ועשה טוב—turn away from evil and do good," which means we're supposed to do just the opposite, that before we can achieve holiness, we must purify ourselves, or we will not be able to do good.

Chazal liken people who try to achieve holiness without purity as "טובל ושרץ בידו—one who immerses with an impure creature in hand." People like this cannot become pure, no matter how often they immerse themselves, because the source of their impurity is not being released! They must first get rid of the evil—סור מרע. Only then can they pursue their quest for good.

Why then, asked HaGaon HaRav Moshe Feinstein zt"l, do we first do קדש, where we achieve holiness, and only then purify ourselves with ורחץ?

The answer is that, unfortunately, many people who perform mitzvos also do aveiros. It is much easier for such people to engage in the pursuit of holiness than to purify themselves by getting rid of the evil.

Urechatz

We wash our hands, but do not recite the customary blessing.

♦ פירוש ♦

Therefore, we engage them in קדש first. After they have been involved in holiness they are ready for ורחץ—purification.

♦ ♦ ♦ ♦ ♦ ♦

We are in the midst of an era of spiritual growth. Torah is flourishing, our yeshivos are full, and many lost Jews are returning to the ways of their ancestors.

At the same time, we are faced with the challenge of young boys and girls who have strayed. Getting them to return to yiddishkeit is a task that must be met with sensitivity, understanding, and much *siyata d'Shmaya* (unprecedented Divine assistance).

Sometimes, when we try to bring back these youth who have strayed, we must first encourage them to do some active mitzvos before they have even "washed themselves" (ורחץ) of the aveiros with which they are involved. One example of this is a despondent couple who discussed their son's spiritual downslide with me. While we were talking about what they could do to help their son, I also asked them if they had recently checked their tefillin and mezuzos. They were astonished by my remark.

"We were just in Eretz Yisroel," they said. "A gadol there told us to do all we could to get our son to wear tefillin.

"Tefillin?" we said, surprised. "The boy is involved in so many terrible sins. How will tefillin help him?"

The rabbi explained that the mitzvah of tefillin is so powerful, it could influence a wayward Jewish boy to perform more mitzvos, bringing him back to the proper path.

Indeed, the young man had stopped wearing tefillin. But with patience, understanding and gentle guidance, he was slowly drawn back to the mitzvah of tefillin.

כַּרְפַּס

The Seder leader dips a vegetable into saltwater, distributes small portions of it to all assembled, and, before eating it, all recite the following blessing:

בָּרוּךְ אַתָּה יְיָ, אֱלֹהֵינוּ מֶלֶךְ הָעוֹלָם, בּוֹרֵא פְּרִי הָאֲדָמָה:

When reciting the blessing, keep in mind the marror (bitter herbs) since this blessing applies also to the marror.

◆ פ י ר ו ש ◆

Our lives are affected directly by many different factors. Some revealed, others hidden. The mezuzos of our house have a lot to do with our mazal and our protection. Therefore, when things go inexplicably awry, it has been our mesorah over the years to examine the kashrus of our tefillin and mezuzos. Often the exact point of invalidation on a mezuzah or tefillin may directly correspond to the problem at hand.

The tefillin itself are a special sign given to us by Hashem. Tefillin make a profound impact on the person. The tefillin of the head will influence a man's direction in life. With this boy, just the wearing of the tefillin triggered a powerful feeling. Tefillin have a subliminal influence so it was helpful for him just to put them on—even if he still didn't daven and his heart was not yet into it. He slowly started to come back and has reached a level where he is now rejoining his family and returning to the derech.

◆ ◆ ◆ ◆ ◆ ◆

The *Sefer HaChinuch* writes that each Jewish male, even if he is impure or has sinned, is obligated to wear tefillin. Tefillin serve as a reminder of Hashem's sovereignty and of men's obligations as Jews. Hopefully, the mitzvah will propel even the most alienated Jewish male to abandon his ways (ורחץ)—even his idol worship—and return to the ways of the Torah (קדש).

I have been asked advice numerous times concerning possible approaches to use for youth who have strayed from the path of Torah and mitzvos, and actually the concepts of tefillin have importance for everyone.

Karpas

The Seder leader dips a vegetable into saltwater, distributes small portions of it to all assembled, and, before eating it, all recite the following blessing:

Blessed are You, Hashem, our God, King of the universe, Who creates the fruit of the soil.

When reciting the blessing, keep in mind the marror (bitter herbs) since this blessing applies also to the marror.

♦ פ י ר ו ש ♦

It is interesting that the tzaddik, R' Levi Yitzchok of Berditchev, also known as the Berditchever, pointed out that the term for "tefillin of the head" (tefillin shel rosh) used in halacha is "tefillin sheb'rosh"; literally, "tefillin *in* the head."

The Berditchever says the reason for this distinction is that merely wearing tefillin *on* the head is not enough; the mitzvah requires incorporating the *concept* of tefillin. Hashem's oneness and the tenets of faith that are contained within the tefillin must be deeply ingrained upon the neshomoh, and we must constantly keep these mitzvos in mind. Therefore, it says "tefillin sheb'rosh," because the tefillin must be figuratively worn *in* the head.

Understanding this, we see that we all have a connection with the mitzvah of tefillin—both men and women. By talking about the concepts contained in the mitzvah of tefillin and speaking sensitively to a young person's heart, it's possible to accomplish a great deal with one's words. As our Chazal tell us, "דברים היוצאים מן הלב נכנסים אל הלב—words that emanate from the heart penetrate the heart."

♦ ♦ ♦ ♦ ♦ ♦

כַּרְפַּס

What is the significance of karpas? The Aleksander Rebbe, who wrote a classic commentary on the Torah called *Yismach Yisrael*, explains: The Jews in Egypt can be likened to the vegetable of karpas. How does a vegetable come

The middle matzah is broken in two. The smaller piece is placed between the other two matzos on the Seder plate, and the larger piece is put away to be eaten later as the afikomen.

פירוש

to be? From a hole in the earth, the seed begins to sprout. It grows and develops, and finally pierces the ground, growing into a beautiful vegetable.

So too, our ancestors were buried in the mire of Egyptian immorality, deep in the dirt of idolatry and impurity. But from the depths of that impurity, the Jewish nation began to develop, eventually piercing the darkness and reaching the greatest spiritual pinnacles.

In our times, too, we may feel we have reached a morass so deep, there can be nothing beyond it. But we should not despair. Hashem has helped us in the past, and He will help again. Hashem can send salvation in the blink of an eye, and from the depths the unfortunate can rise to lofty heights. So just as the karpas emerges from its humble origins one day to find itself on the table of kings, so too can Jews emerge from darkness and ascend to great heights.

♦ ♦ ♦ ♦ ♦ ♦

מַגִּיד

The Maharal underscores that the *avodah* of *leil* Pesach is "the mouth that speaks"—relating and telling over of the story of *yetzias Mitzrayim* to our children. This, of course, is a מצוה דאורייתא, the source being: "ולמען תספר באזני בנך ובן בנך...—and so that you may relate in the ears of your son and your son's son" (Shemos 12).

Two insightful questions are asked on this posuk. Why does it say "באזני—in the ears"? Human's have only one mode of listening in this world and this is with our ears. The second question is, if the mitzvah is that parents relate the story to their own children, then it stands to reason that in the future the children will one day be parents and have the mitzvah to relate it to their children. It would therefore suffice to tell

Yachatz

The middle matzah is broken in two. The smaller piece is placed between the other two matzos on the Seder plate, and the larger piece is put away to be eaten later as the afikomen.

♦ פ י ר ו ש ♦

the story of yetzias Mitzrayim to the children, and then let the children relate it to their children.

The answer is "באזני" means that our comments must be tailored so that they can be accepted by a listener's ears. Not every child can hear the same amount, understand the same depth, or absorb the same words. Secondly, when we relate the message of the Haggadah, it has to be done in such a way that the children listening will be so affected that they will excitedly await the opportunity to share this information with their future children.

♦ ♦ ♦ ♦ ♦ ♦

כָּל דִּכְפִין יֵיתֵי וְיֵכוֹל...לְשָׁנָה הַבָּאָה בְּנֵי חוֹרִין

Let all who are hungry come and eat...Next year, may we be free.

How is our invitation to the hungry to join us connected with our hope that next year we will be free?

"ציון במשפט תפדה ושביה בצדקה—Zion will be redeemed with justice, and her captives, with charity" (Yeshaya 1:27). When we do acts of charity, such as inviting poor people to eat with us, we hope that this merit will allow us to be redeemed, and next year we will, in fact, be free. Furthermore, the Gemarah (Bava Basra 10a) tells us, "Tzedakah is great, because it will hasten the redemption."

Charity is so crucial that its merit can bring the geulah!

♦ ♦ ♦ ♦ ♦ ♦

The importance of tzedakah and chesed is illustrated by the following: HaGaon HaRav Elazar Menachem Mann Shach zt"l asked: Why doesn't the Torah tell us all of the wondrous tales of Avraham Avinu that we hear

מַגִּיד

We now recite the narrative portion of the Haggadah, which describes the suffering we endured while enslaved in Egypt and how God freed us from bondage and took us out of Egypt. During the recital of the following paragraph, the seder plate is lifted and the matzos are uncovered.

הָא לַחְמָא עַנְיָא דִּי אֲכָלוּ אַבְהָתָנָא בְּאַרְעָא דְמִצְרָיִם. כָּל דִּכְפִין יֵיתֵי וְיֵכוֹל, כָּל דִּצְרִיךְ יֵיתֵי וְיִפְסַח. הָשַׁתָּא הָכָא, לְשָׁנָה הַבָּאָה בְּאַרְעָא דְיִשְׂרָאֵל. הָשַׁתָּא עַבְדֵי, לְשָׁנָה הַבָּאָה בְּנֵי חוֹרִין:

♦ פ י ר ו ש ♦

about in Midrash? Why is there no direct mention in the Torah of Avraham's *mesiras nefesh* in fighting idolatry? Even the astonishing miracle of Avraham's salvation from the burning furnace is merely hinted at, and elaborated upon only in Midrash! But Avraham Avinu's chesed is discussed in detail. Although Avraham Avinu's chesed is surely incredible—it's not miraculous. And yet, the Torah devotes many words to tell us about it. Why?

Clearly, Avraham's chesed was more noteworthy than the miraculous tales of his success in breaking his father's idols, and even more extraordinary than his deliverance from Nimrod's fiery furnace!

When we invite the poor to our Seder table, we are emulating Avraham Avinu's chesed—and, by doing this, we hasten the coming of Moshiach. This is why we can voice our hope for freedom *after* we invite the poor and say "Let all who are hungry come...": Redemption has, indeed, come closer.

♦ ♦ ♦ ♦ ♦ ♦

Why is this invitation to the poor after kiddush? If they are our guests shouldn't they be invited at the Seder's start, so that they, too, can hear kiddush?

The Torah, source of all wisdom, plumbs the depths of the human

Maggid

We now recite the narrative portion of the Haggadah, which describes the suffering we endured while enslaved in Egypt and how God freed us from bondage and took us out of Egypt. During the recital of the following paragraph, the seder plate is lifted and the matzos are uncovered.

This is the poor bread that our forefathers ate in the land of Egypt. Let all who are hungry come and eat. Let all who are needy come and celebrate the Pesach festival. Now we are here. Next year may we be in the land of Israel! Now we are slaves. Next year may we all be free!

♦ פ י ר ו ש ♦

psyche. People who are poor suffer from more than lack of money; they also feel enormous shame. That is why a poor, lonely man may stay in shul long after everyone has gone home Pesach night. He stares with longing at the well-lit homes, where he can view groups of people sitting down to their well-set Seder tables. It takes him time to gain courage to approach a home and ask to join the Seder.

That is why our invitation is extended after kiddush, when we can expect the poor to stand at our doors, waiting to be asked inside.

It is best to find a way for a poor person to come inside without wounding his or her pride. The posuk (Tehillim 41:2) tells us, "אשרי משכיל אל דל—fortunate is one who uses wisdom to help the poor." Those who do so are treading the path of Avraham Avinu, who sat at פתח האוהל (in the door of his tent), waiting for wayfarers and quickly inviting them inside, easing their plight by even eliminating their need to ask to be invited.

♦ ♦ ♦ ♦ ♦ ♦

מַה נִּשְׁתַּנָּה הַלַּיְלָה הַזֶּה מִכָּל הַלֵּילוֹת?

R' Levi Yitzchok of Berditchev noted: Hashem waits for us to ask the "מה נשתנה..., Why is this 'night' different?" The "night" also being symbolic of our

The matzos are covered again, and the Seder plate is removed.
The second cup of wine is poured. Now the youngest child present asks:

מַה נִּשְׁתַּנָּה הַלַּיְלָה הַזֶּה מִכָּל הַלֵּילוֹת?

שֶׁבְּכָל הַלֵּילוֹת אָנוּ אוֹכְלִין חָמֵץ וּמַצָּה.
הַלַּיְלָה הַזֶּה כֻּלּוֹ מַצָּה:

שֶׁבְּכָל הַלֵּילוֹת אָנוּ אוֹכְלִין שְׁאָר יְרָקוֹת,
הַלַּיְלָה הַזֶּה מָרוֹר:

שֶׁבְּכָל הַלֵּילוֹת אֵין אָנוּ מַטְבִּילִין אֲפִילוּ פַּעַם אֶחָת.
הַלַּיְלָה הַזֶּה שְׁתֵּי פְעָמִים:

שֶׁבְּכָל הַלֵּילוֹת אָנוּ אוֹכְלִין בֵּין יוֹשְׁבִין וּבֵין מְסֻבִּין.
הַלַּיְלָה הַזֶּה כֻּלָּנוּ מְסֻבִּין:

◆ פ י ר ו ש ◆

long night of galus. It's a reminder for us to ask: Why is this galus so long? Why have we been exiled for so many years more than the other exiles?

When Hashem hears us questioning, expressing our yearning for the end of galus, He sends His blessings upon us, which will hasten the redemption.

◆ ◆ ◆ ◆ ◆ ◆

What is so different about this night, the night of galus? Rav Shlomo Efraim, the 16th century author of the *Ollelos Efraim* asked. Why has this exile lasted so much longer than our other exiles?

The reason is because הלילה הזה כלו מצה—this exile has been filled with מצה ומריבה, both strife and disunity. It says in Yeshayahu (58:4): לריב ומצה תצומו—because you fast for grievance and strife." Because dispute and baseless hatred exist in the world, our galus has been prolonged.

◆ ◆ ◆ ◆ ◆ ◆

The renowned 18th century gaon, kabbalist and posek, the Ben Ish Chai

The matzos are covered again, and the Seder plate is removed. The second cup of wine is poured.

Now the youngest child present asks:

Why is this night different from all other nights?

On all other nights, we eat both bread and matzah,
but on this night only matzah.

On all other nights we eat all types of herbs,
but on this night we eat marror (bitter herbs).

On all other nights, we do not dip even once,
but on this night we dip twice.

On all other nights, we eat either sitting or reclining,
but on this night we all recline.

♦ פירוש ♦

comments: Children usually ask questions about the things they are told they are not allowed to do. It is not difficult to understand why they ask about matzah, with all of its restrictions; marror, with its inherent bitterness; and karpas, where we do something different by eating less than a kezayis. But the Ben Ish Chai asks: why would a child ask about reclining? Isn't freedom something a child naturally likes to exhibit?

In a response indicative of the nature of children, the Ben Ish Chai responds, "To children, freedom is doing what they want to do. They want to eat in the position of their choice. If we tell them to recline, we have interfered with their freedom—and so, they question."

♦ ♦ ♦ ♦ ♦ ♦

עֲבָדִים הָיִינוּ...וְאִלּוּ לֹא הוֹצִיא הַקָּדוֹשׁ בָּרוּךְ הוּא אֶת אֲבוֹתֵינוּ מִמִּצְרַיִם

HaGaon HaRav Aaron Kotler zt"l, in his sefer *Mishnas Reb Aharon*, asks: Would we, indeed, still be enslaved in Mitzrayim today, after so many years, had Hashem not taken us out when He did?

We must take note of the difference in terminology the Baal Haggadah uses. When the Haggadah discusses our state in Egypt, it says

The matzos are now uncovered, and the Seder leader replies, accompanied by the entire assembly:

עֲבָדִים הָיִינוּ לְפַרְעֹה בְּמִצְרָיִם. וַיּוֹצִיאֵנוּ יְיָ אֱלֹהֵינוּ מִשָּׁם, בְּיָד חֲזָקָה וּבִזְרוֹעַ נְטוּיָה, וְאִלּוּ לֹא הוֹצִיא הַקָּדוֹשׁ בָּרוּךְ הוּא אֶת אֲבוֹתֵינוּ מִמִּצְרַיִם, הֲרֵי אָנוּ וּבָנֵינוּ וּבְנֵי בָנֵינוּ, מְשֻׁעְבָּדִים הָיִינוּ לְפַרְעֹה בְּמִצְרָיִם. וַאֲפִילוּ כֻּלָּנוּ חֲכָמִים, כֻּלָּנוּ נְבוֹנִים, כֻּלָּנוּ זְקֵנִים, כֻּלָּנוּ יוֹדְעִים אֶת הַתּוֹרָה, מִצְוָה עָלֵינוּ לְסַפֵּר בִּיצִיאַת מִצְרָיִם. וְכָל הַמַּרְבֶּה לְסַפֵּר בִּיצִיאַת מִצְרַיִם, הֲרֵי זֶה מְשֻׁבָּח:

◆ פירוש ◆

"עבדים היינו—we were slaves." Later, when the Haggadah talks about what our current state would be had we not been redeemed, it uses the term "משעובדים—enslaved."

We may, indeed, have been released from our bondage at some point—but it would have been a physical release. Spiritually, however, we would have remained enslaved to Pharaoh; to his immorality and his corruption. In order to emerge from our desperate spiritual situation, we needed *siyata d'Shmaya* (unprecedented Divine assistance).

Today, too, we must pray for Divine assistance in spiritual matters. We must not make the mistake of thinking we can escape the depths of depravity surrounding us merely by will. Instead, we must pray for constant *siyata d'Shmaya*, and for deliverance from our spiritual exile.

◆ ◆ ◆ ◆ ◆ ◆

וְאִלּוּ לֹא הוֹצִיא הַקָּדוֹשׁ בָּרוּךְ הוּא אֶת אֲבוֹתֵינוּ
...הֲרֵי אָנוּ וּבָנֵינוּ...מְשֻׁעְבָּדִים הָיִינוּ לְפַרְעֹה

If Pharaoh had granted us freedom, we would be forever indebted to him. But only Hashem could have freed us, and we must thank only Him for the geulah.

The matzos are now uncovered, and the Seder leader replies, accompanied by the entire assembly:

We were slaves to Pharaoh in Egypt, and Hashem, our God took us out of there with a mighty hand and an outstretched arm. And if the Holy One, blessed be He, had not taken our fathers out of Egypt, then we, our children, and our children's children would still be enslaved to Pharaoh in Egypt. And even if we were all wise, all full of understanding, all advanced in years, all knowledgeable of the Torah, it still would be incumbent upon us to tell about the Exodus from Egypt. And the more one tells of the Exodus from Egypt, the more praiseworthy one is.

In all aspects of life, we must remember that all of the good we experience, and all of our deliverances, come only from Hashem. We should never think "כחי ועוצם ידי עשה לי את החיל הזה—My strength has brought me this good" (Devarim 8:17). Rather, we should continually thank Hashem, and recognize that everything we have is from Him.

♦ ♦ ♦ ♦ ♦ ♦

Rav Shamshon Raphael Hirsch comments: When Hashem foretold to Avraham Avinu of the slavery in Egypt three characteristics of the future slavery were alluded to: "Your children will be a stranger in a land that is not theirs, they will enslave them and afflict them for four hundred years" (Bereishis 14:13). Here we see *geirus*—that we were aliens without rights; *avdus*—we were enslaved and powerless to utilize our capabilities; and *inuy*—our bodies were physically afflicted.

There are three parts to the prohibiton of eating chametz, each directly corresponding to the three aspects of slavery from which Hashem freed us: Not to eat chametz, which indicates that our bodies and our needs are dedicated to Hashem; not to derive use from chametz, demonstrates that it was through Hashem that we are able to use our capabilities; lastly, we do not keep any chametz in our possession, to make it clear that all that we have comes from Hashem and belongs to Him.

מַעֲשֶׂה בְּרַבִּי אֱלִיעֶזֶר, וְרַבִּי יְהוֹשֻׁעַ, וְרַבִּי אֶלְעָזָר בֶּן עֲזַרְיָה, וְרַבִּי עֲקִיבָא, וְרַבִּי טַרְפוֹן, שֶׁהָיוּ מְסֻבִּין בִּבְנֵי בְרַק, וְהָיוּ מְסַפְּרִים בִּיצִיאַת מִצְרַיִם, כָּל אוֹתוֹ הַלַּיְלָה, עַד שֶׁבָּאוּ תַלְמִידֵיהֶם וְאָמְרוּ לָהֶם: רַבּוֹתֵינוּ, הִגִּיעַ זְמַן קְרִיאַת שְׁמַע שֶׁל שַׁחֲרִית:

◆ פ י ר ו ש ◆

מַעֲשֶׂה בְּרַבִּי אֱלִיעֶזֶר...שֶׁהָיוּ מְסֻבִּין בִּבְנֵי בְרַק

How is it that these brilliant tzaddikim did not sense that morning had already arrived, until their students alerted them to the fact?

The Seder of these giants was held in one of the gloomiest eras in Jewish history. The Romans had forbidden the practice of Judaism, and Jews were being forced to convert. And so the five most extraordinary rabbis of the time were compelled to conduct their Seder in a cave—hidden from the probing eyes of the Roman army. They were unexposed to any source of sunlight, and had no way of knowing that the day had dawned.

Today in America, when we can celebrate the Seder and openly practice the entire Torah fearlessly, we must heighten our awareness of our privilege, and observe Torah and mitzvos with immense joy, as is movingly illustrated in the following story.

A Jewish man who emigrated from Russia to the United States would bring his son to yeshiva each day. This was not unusual, except that his son was seventeen years old, and quite able to travel by himself! When asked why he escorted his teenager, he happily explained.

"In Russia, I refused to send my son to public school, because I knew that he would be taught to deny all things Jewish. Now that we live here, my son goes to yeshiva. I am so thrilled, I want to witness his entering the yeshiva building every day!"

◆ ◆ ◆ ◆ ◆ ◆

הִגִּיעַ זְמַן קְרִיאַת שְׁמַע שֶׁל שַׁחֲרִית

Our Chachomim ask: Why "Shacharis"? Why not Mincha or Maariv?

It is told that Rabbi Eliezer, Rabbi Joshua, Rabbi Elazar ben Azariah, Rabbi Akiva, and Rabbi Tarfon were reclining together at a seder in Bnei Brak. They spoke of the Exodus from Egypt throughout the night, until their disciples came and said to them, "Our Masters, it is time to recite the morning Shema."

◆ פ י ר ו ש ◆

We find many places in Shas that when tzaddikim were engaged in Torah, a tremendous light would surround them. Certainly we would have to say that when these brilliant talmidim were learning a bright light illuminated the room, which seemed to be just like the morning sun. They had no idea whether it was their own light they were experiencing or the morning light.

The Maharash built a large house which included many tall, wide windows. The Tzemach Tzedek asked him, "Why do you need such big windows?" The Maharash answered, "In order for the house to be well lit."

The Tzemach Tzedek responded, "By the zeide there were no windows at all!" The Maharash said, "So it must have been dark." The Tzemach Tzedek exclaimed, "On the contrary, *gevald* it was *lichtig*! (Indeed it was full of light!)"

◆ ◆ ◆ ◆ ◆ ◆

אָמַר רַבִּי אֶלְעָזָר

The Chachomim tell us that the words "ימי חייך—the days of your life" refer to Olam Hazeh, and that "כל ימי חייך—all of the days of your life," refer to the days of Moshiach.

The Vilna Gaon teaches that this is a proof to what Chazal tell us about the nachash (the serpent). Chazal say that when Moshiach comes, everyone but the nachash will be healed: "לעתיד לבא הכל מתרפאים חוץ מן הנחש." The nachash will still be bound to the curse he earned on the first day of his existence.

When Hashem cursed the serpent, He said, "עפר תאכל כל ימי חייך—You

אָמַר רַבִּי אֶלְעָזָר בֶּן עֲזַרְיָה. הֲרֵי אֲנִי כְּבֶן שִׁבְעִים שָׁנָה, וְלֹא זָכִיתִי, שֶׁתֵּאָמֵר יְצִיאַת מִצְרַיִם בַּלֵּילוֹת. עַד שֶׁדְּרָשָׁהּ בֶּן זוֹמָא. שֶׁנֶּאֱמַר: לְמַעַן תִּזְכֹּר, אֶת יוֹם צֵאתְךָ מֵאֶרֶץ מִצְרַיִם, כֹּל יְמֵי חַיֶּיךָ. יְמֵי חַיֶּיךָ הַיָּמִים. כֹּל יְמֵי חַיֶּיךָ הַלֵּילוֹת. וַחֲכָמִים אוֹמְרִים: יְמֵי חַיֶּיךָ הָעוֹלָם הַזֶּה. כֹּל יְמֵי חַיֶּיךָ לְהָבִיא לִימוֹת הַמָּשִׁיחַ:

בָּרוּךְ הַמָּקוֹם. בָּרוּךְ הוּא. בָּרוּךְ שֶׁנָּתַן תּוֹרָה לְעַמּוֹ יִשְׂרָאֵל. בָּרוּךְ הוּא כְּנֶגֶד אַרְבָּעָה בָנִים דִּבְּרָה תוֹרָה. אֶחָד חָכָם, וְאֶחָד רָשָׁע, וְאֶחָד תָּם, וְאֶחָד שֶׁאֵינוֹ יוֹדֵעַ לִשְׁאוֹל:

♦ פ י ר ו ש ♦

will eat dust all of the days of your life." As in the Haggadah, the Vilna Gaon says, כל ימי חייך refers to the days of Moshiach, for even then the serpent will eat dust.

Why will the nachash continue to suffer while the rest of the world enjoys healing and good health? It is because of the sin he committed by telling lashon hara about Hashem! Naturally, the nachash didn't receive the gift of being able to do teshuva. We, on the other hand, have the Divine gift of being able to do teshuva even for aveiros as grave as lashon hara.

♦ ♦ ♦ ♦ ♦ ♦

כֹּל יְמֵי חַיֶּיךָ לְהָבִיא לִימוֹת הַמָּשִׁיח

Besides for their literal translation, these words also teach us about one of our most important obligations. We must know that "all the days of your life," means that as long as we live, we are obligated to hope, yearn, and pray, "to hasten the coming of Moshiach"—for the redemption.

When we face the Beis Din shel Maalah (the Heavenly Court), one

Rabbi Elazar ben Azariah said: "I am like a man of seventy, yet I have never succeeded in proving that the Exodus from Egypt should be mentioned at night, until Ben Zoma explained it—for it is written, 'That you should remember the day you came forth from Egypt all the days of your life' (Devarim 16:3). 'The days of your life' implies that we must mention it only during the days. 'All the days of your life,' however, includes the nights as well. The Sages, however, explain that 'the days of your life' implies that we must mention the Exodus only in the present world. 'All the days of your life' refers to the time of the Messiah as well."

Blessed be the Ever-Present, blessed be He. Blessed be He Who gave the Torah to His people Israel, blessed be He. The Torah speaks of four sons: one wise, one wicked, one simple, and one who does not know how to ask.

◆ פירוש ◆

of the questions we will be asked is "צפית לישועה? Did you await the redemption?" Why is this so important?

Many tzaddikim teach that even our yearning plays a significant role in the geulah. One who yearns for redemption is actually bringing it closer. It is, therefore, a serious obligation on the part of every Jew to actively yearn and hope for the geulah.

◆ ◆ ◆ ◆ ◆ ◆

בָּרוּךְ הַמָּקוֹם. בָּרוּךְ הוּא.

Why does the Haggadah use the name מקום, rather than any of the other names usually used for Hakadosh Baruch Hu?

The answer is because we are speaking to all four sons. The תם might think that Hashem is with the *chochom*, because he learns Torah. The *rashah* might feel that Hashem is with all of the sons but him, because he has sinned.

The Baal Haggadah is telling all Jewish boys and girls that, no matter where they may be in life, they can find Hashem. Even the *rashah* can find Hashem, for Hashem is המקום—ubiquitous, in every place, at every

חָכָם מַה הוּא אוֹמֵר? מָה הָעֵדֹת וְהַחֻקִּים וְהַמִּשְׁפָּטִים, אֲשֶׁר צִוָּה יְיָ אֱלֹהֵינוּ אֶתְכֶם? וְאַף אַתָּה אֱמָר לוֹ כְּהִלְכוֹת הַפֶּסַח: אֵין מַפְטִירִין אַחַר הַפֶּסַח אֲפִיקוֹמָן:

רָשָׁע מַה הוּא אוֹמֵר? מָה הָעֲבֹדָה הַזֹּאת לָכֶם? לָכֶם וְלֹא לוֹ. וּלְפִי שֶׁהוֹצִיא אֶת עַצְמוֹ מִן הַכְּלָל, כָּפַר בָּעִקָּר. וְאַף אַתָּה הַקְהֵה אֶת שִׁנָּיו, וֶאֱמָר לוֹ: בַּעֲבוּר זֶה, עָשָׂה יְיָ לִי, בְּצֵאתִי מִמִּצְרָיִם, לִי וְלֹא לוֹ. אִלּוּ הָיָה שָׁם, לֹא הָיָה נִגְאָל:

פ י ר ו ש

time, and Hashem listens to those who cry out to Him, regardless of their merits (זכויות).

♦ ♦ ♦ ♦ ♦ ♦

כְּנֶגֶד אַרְבָּעָה בָנִים דִּבְּרָה תוֹרָה

We are not allowed to ignore a Jewish child. All children, whether he or she is wise, wicked, or foolish, even the one who does not know to question, is entitled, and must receive an answer. And not just any answer must be given; answers must be custom-tailored to each child's nature and ability.

This is the definition of "חנוך לנער על פי דרכו—train the child according to his or her way," says the brilliant 19th century thinker, Rabbi Shamshon Rafael Hirsch. Before answering a child, parents are obligated to first examine each child individually, looking at their nature, ability, and level of understanding, and answer each question accordingly. A single approach to all children is *not* chinuch.

♦ ♦ ♦ ♦ ♦ ♦

אֶחָד חָכָם, וְאֶחָד רָשָׁע

The Satmar Rav zt"l, in *Divrei Yoel*, asks: Why do we say אחד חכם אחד

The wise son, what does he say? "What are the testimonies, the laws, and the ordinances that Hashem, our God, has commanded you?" (Devarim 6:2). Tell him of all the laws of Pesach—including ing that one may not eat any dessert after the Paschal offering.

The wicked son, what does he say? "What is this service to you?" By saying "to you" he excludes himself from the community. By excluding himself, he has denied a fundamental principle of our faith. Therefore, you must cause him distress, by stating, "Because of this, Hashem did this for me when I came out of Egypt" (Shemos 12:26). For me, but not for him. Had he been there, he would not have been redeemed.

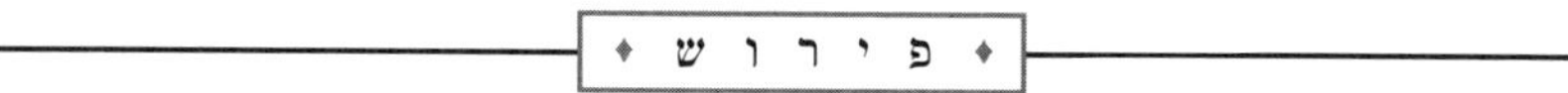

רשע—one is *wise* and one is evil? A more appropriate opposition would be to say אחד צדיק אחד רשע—one is righteous and one is evil.

The Rebbe explains that in dealing with a *rashah*, it is not enough to be a tzaddik; one must be a *chochom* to battle the devious and cunning *rashah*, and put the *rashah* in place.

חָכָם מַה הוּא אוֹמֵר?

The fact that the evil son is listed right after the wise son speaks power fully:

- His proximity to the wise son is a source of encouragement to the *rashah*. He is just one step away from being the *chochom*.
- The wise son is admonished to take care of his evil brother. כל ישראל ערבים זה לזה—All Jews bear responsibility for each other. It is the *chochom*'s obligation to bring his estranged brother back to a Torah life.
- It is a warning to the *chochom*—don't fall into the trap of complacency. Don't be self-assured in your status as a *chochom*, for you are only one short step away from the *rashah*. In order to retain your footing, you must continue to grow, for lack of growth can cause you to stumble to the depths of the evil son.

תָּם מַה הוּא אוֹמֵר? מַה זֹּאת? וְאָמַרְתָּ אֵלָיו: בְּחֹזֶק יָד הוֹצִיאָנוּ יְיָ מִמִּצְרַיִם מִבֵּית עֲבָדִים:

וְשֶׁאֵינוֹ יוֹדֵעַ לִשְׁאוֹל, אַתְּ פְּתַח לוֹ. שֶׁנֶּאֱמַר: וְהִגַּדְתָּ לְבִנְךָ, בַּיּוֹם הַהוּא לֵאמֹר: בַּעֲבוּר זֶה עָשָׂה יְיָ לִי, בְּצֵאתִי מִמִּצְרָיִם:

יָכוֹל מֵרֹאשׁ חֹדֶשׁ, תַּלְמוּד לוֹמַר בַּיּוֹם הַהוּא. אִי בַּיּוֹם הַהוּא. יָכוֹל מִבְּעוֹד יוֹם. תַּלְמוּד לוֹמַר. בַּעֲבוּר זֶה. בַּעֲבוּר זֶה לֹא אָמַרְתִּי, אֶלָּא בְּשָׁעָה שֶׁיֵּשׁ מַצָּה וּמָרוֹר מֻנָּחִים לְפָנֶיךָ:

◆ פ י ר ו ש ◆

רָשָׁע מַה הוּא אוֹמֵר? מָה הָעֲבֹדָה הַזֹּאת לָכֶם...הַקְהֵה אֶת שִׁנָּיו

The Baal Haggadah tells us how to reply to the *rashah*—knock his teeth out! Why?

The Kozhnitzer Maggid, an 18th century leader and chasidic Rebbe who had a profound influence on the Jewish world, explains: A *rashah*'s idea of Judaism is that Hashem can be served only with Torah and prayer i.e., with spiritual pursuits. He denies that our *avodas* Hashem consists of all of our actions ברוחניות ובגשמיות (spiritually and physically), including eating and drinking, etc., which is why we knock his teeth out: If he believes that one cannot serve Hashem through the act of eating, he doesn't need his teeth!

◆ ◆ ◆ ◆ ◆ ◆

שֶׁאֵינוֹ יוֹדֵעַ לִשְׁאוֹל

There is no need to question Hashem when we have emunah, says the Klausenberger Rebbe zt"l, who was a chasidic world leader . We become a "שאינו יודע לשאול—the child who does not know to ask." We don't question Hashem's ways; we accept everything with pure and deeply felt faith.

The simple son, what does he say? He says "What is this?" You should say to him, "With a mighty hand did Hashem take us out of Egypt, out of the house of bondage" (Shemos 13:14).

As for the son who does not know how to ask, you should initiate the discussion with him, as it is stated, "And you should tell your child on that day, saying: 'Because of this, Hashem did this did for me when I came out of Egypt'" (Shemos 13:8).

One might think that the duty to discuss the Exodus begins on the new moon of Nissan. The Torah, therefore, says "on that day." The expression "on that day" suggests that this discussion should take place in the daytime; therefore, the Torah says "because of this" which implies that the discussion should take place only when matzah and bitter herbs are placed before you.

♦ פירוש ♦

Our reward is את פתח לו—the Ribono Shel Olam opens the Gates of Heaven and the Gates of Torah, and gives us all we need, from א to ת—from beginning to end.

♦ ♦ ♦ ♦ ♦ ♦

מִתְּחִלָּה עוֹבְדֵי עֲבוֹדָה זָרָה הָיוּ אֲבוֹתֵינוּ

Rabbi Eliyahu Dessler wrote in his sefer, *Michtav Me'Eliyahu,* Why do we start the Haggadah by remembering our idol-worshipping ancestors? Couldn't the Haggadah have instead recounted Avraham Avinu and the tremendous yichus he began? What's the point of recalling this unsavory part of our history?

Rabbi Dessler explains that we start with this to remind ourselves of Avraham's extraordinary strength and perseverance. Avraham Avinu rose against immense odds to fight the entire world's ideology, bring Hashem's glory to this world of idolatry, and become the father of the Jewish People.

What a lesson to us! How often are we challenged with a test of right against wrong? We must learn from Avraham Avinu. We must resist the

מִתְּחִלָּה עוֹבְדֵי עֲבוֹדָה זָרָה הָיוּ אֲבוֹתֵינוּ. וְעַכְשָׁו קֵרְבָנוּ הַמָּקוֹם לַעֲבוֹדָתוֹ. שֶׁנֶּאֱמַר: וַיֹּאמֶר יְהוֹשֻׁעַ אֶל כָּל הָעָם. כֹּה אָמַר יְיָ אֱלֹהֵי יִשְׂרָאֵל, בְּעֵבֶר הַנָּהָר יָשְׁבוּ אֲבוֹתֵיכֶם מֵעוֹלָם, תֶּרַח אֲבִי אַבְרָהָם וַאֲבִי נָחוֹר. וַיַּעַבְדוּ אֱלֹהִים אֲחֵרִים: וָאֶקַּח אֶת אֲבִיכֶם אֶת אַבְרָהָם מֵעֵבֶר הַנָּהָר, וָאוֹלֵךְ אוֹתוֹ בְּכָל אֶרֶץ כְּנָעַן. וָאַרְבֶּה אֶת זַרְעוֹ, וָאֶתֶּן לוֹ אֶת יִצְחָק: וָאֶתֵּן לְיִצְחָק אֶת יַעֲקֹב וְאֶת עֵשָׂו. וָאֶתֵּן לְעֵשָׂו אֶת הַר שֵׂעִיר לָרֶשֶׁת אוֹתוֹ. וְיַעֲקֹב וּבָנָיו יָרְדוּ מִצְרָיִם:

בָּרוּךְ שׁוֹמֵר הַבְטָחָתוֹ לְיִשְׂרָאֵל. בָּרוּךְ הוּא. שֶׁהַקָּדוֹשׁ בָּרוּךְ הוּא חִשַּׁב אֶת הַקֵּץ, לַעֲשׂוֹת כְּמָה שֶׁאָמַר לְאַבְרָהָם אָבִינוּ בִּבְרִית בֵּין הַבְּתָרִים, שֶׁנֶּאֱמַר: וַיֹּאמֶר לְאַבְרָם יָדֹעַ תֵּדַע, כִּי גֵר יִהְיֶה זַרְעֲךָ, בְּאֶרֶץ לֹא לָהֶם, וַעֲבָדוּם וְעִנּוּ אֹתָם אַרְבַּע מֵאוֹת שָׁנָה: וְגַם אֶת הַגּוֹי אֲשֶׁר יַעֲבֹדוּ דָּן אָנֹכִי. וְאַחֲרֵי כֵן יֵצְאוּ בִּרְכֻשׁ גָּדוֹל:

♦ פ י ר ו ש ♦

temptations that the world and the times present to us; we must search out the truth and persevere in doing what is right.

One person who stood up for his beliefs despite opposition was the Satmar Rebbe zt"l. R' Yoel was only a young bochur of thirteen when he received his rabbinical ordination. There is a well-known episode that occurred not long after his ordination. At a conference at which the entire Satmar community and all of its rabbis were present, a prominent member rose and presented ideas contrary to the Torah perspective. Only the newly ordained future Rebbe stood up and challenged him. Unfazed, the man repeated his suggestion. At this the bochur-rabbi refuted him. The man was still unimpressed. Ignoring the youngster who

In the beginning, our fathers were idol worshipers. Now God has brought us near to His service, as it is written, "And Joshua said to the whole nation: 'Thus said Hashem God of Israel, Your fathers dwelt on the other side of the river from earliest time—Terach, the father of Abraham, and the father of Nachor; and they served other gods. And I took your father Abraham from the other side of the river, and I led him throughout all of the land of Canaan, and I multiplied his seed and gave him Isaac. And to Isaac, I gave Jacob and Esau. To Esau, I gave Mount Seir to inherit it, but Jacob and his children went down into Egypt'" (Yehoshua 24:2-4).

Blessed is He Who keeps His promise to Israel; Blessed is He! For the Holy One, blessed is He, determined the end of the bondage in order to fulfill His promise to Abraham our father in the covenant between the parts, as it is stated, "And He said to Abram: You should surely know that your seed will be strangers in a land not theirs; they will enslave them and oppress them, for four hundred years. But also the nation that they will serve will I judge, and afterward they shall go forth with great wealth" (Bereishis 15:13-14).

♦ פירוש ♦

was challenging him, he continued with his presentation.

R' Yoel could not ignore the man's utter disregard for Torah. Despite the silence of the older rabbonim present, the teenager persevered.

"I am warning you," he said again, standing. "If you do not stop, I, as well as all of the rabbis sitting here, will leave the conference."

The man eyed the young rabbi and sat down.

From an early age, the Satmar Rebbe had been zealous for Hashem's honor. When he heard something improper, he simply could not contain himself and had to speak out. The man had made some liberal statements and had spoken inappropriately. Too many times we let things pass that are wrong. We are complacent. We don't want to make a fuss.

We lift the cup of wine, cover the matzos and recite:

וְהִיא שֶׁעָמְדָה לַאֲבוֹתֵינוּ וְלָנוּ. שֶׁלֹּא אֶחָד בִּלְבָד, עָמַד עָלֵינוּ לְכַלּוֹתֵנוּ. אֶלָּא שֶׁבְּכָל דּוֹר וָדוֹר, עוֹמְדִים עָלֵינוּ לְכַלּוֹתֵנוּ. וְהַקָּדוֹשׁ בָּרוּךְ הוּא מַצִּילֵנוּ מִיָּדָם:

We lower the cup of wine and uncover the matzos.

צֵא וּלְמַד, מַה בִּקֵּשׁ לָבָן הָאֲרַמִּי לַעֲשׂוֹת לְיַעֲקֹב אָבִינוּ. שֶׁפַּרְעֹה לֹא גָזַר אֶלָּא עַל הַזְּכָרִים, וְלָבָן בִּקֵּשׁ לַעֲקֹר אֶת הַכֹּל, שֶׁנֶּאֱמַר: **אֲרַמִּי אֹבֵד אָבִי, וַיֵּרֶד מִצְרַיְמָה, וַיָּגָר שָׁם בִּמְתֵי מְעָט. וַיְהִי שָׁם לְגוֹי גָּדוֹל, עָצוּם וָרָב:**

פ י ר ו ש

But when we hear something that's wrong, we have to speak out for what we believe in. Instead of calculating the risks and seeking to avoid involvement, we must be willing to step forward when necessary.

♦ ♦ ♦ ♦ ♦ ♦

בְּכָל דּוֹר וָדוֹר, עוֹמְדִים עָלֵינוּ לְכַלּוֹתֵנוּ

Why have Jews so often been the target of hate and persecution?

The Baal Shem Tov explains that when a man traveling carries a sack of straw, he treads the roads fearlessly. Highwaymen and other theives would not disturb him, for they have no desire for the worthless straw upon his back.

But a man who carries gold and precious gems has reason to fear. He must be constantly alert for bandits who could rob or murder him for the treasure in his bags.

Jews also carry a priceless load, says the Baal Shem Tov. We bear with pride our yoke of Torah and mitzvos. However, that precious load puts us in a continual state of danger. There are always others only too eager to relieve us of our "bags of jewels" by persecuting us, and even attempting to wipe us off the map.

We lift the cup of wine, cover the matzos and recite:

It is this promise that has sustained our fathers and us, for not only one persecutor has risen up against us to destroy us, but in every generation they rise up against us to destroy us; but the Holy One, blessed is He, delivers us from their hands.

We lower the cup of wine and uncover the matzos.

Go out and learn what Laban the Aramean sought to do to Jacob our father. Whereas Pharaoh decreed death only upon the males, Laban sought to uproot all, as it is stated, ***"An Aramean sought to destroy my father, and he went down to Egypt and sojourned there as a stranger, few in number, and there he became a great nation, strong and numerous"*** (Devarim 26:5).

פירוש

וְהַקָּדוֹשׁ בָּרוּךְ הוּא מַצִּילֵנוּ מִיָּדָם

In his sefer *Esh Kodesh*, Rabbi Kolonymus Kalman, the Rebbe of Pyosetzne, in Poland, asks why the Baal Haggadah uses these words. Wouldn't it have been more correct to say that Hakadosh Baruch Hu saved us "from our enemies"? Why does the Haggadah say, "from their hands"?

It is because the word מידם—from their hands—implies that we were saved even when we were already *in the hands* of our enemies. Even when we were already captured, and the chances of escape seemed remote, through wondrous miracles Hashem helped us.

This is why despair does not exist in Judaism and is actually forbidden: We are a nation that has always survived, and with Hashem's help, we will outlive our enemies—even though we may already be "in their hands."

In times of distress, we must remember that we should not—in fact, we dare not—despair. History has amply demonstrated that even in our darkest hours, the Jews have experienced salvation. It makes little difference if the problem is one of national security or more personal. Hashem's salvation can come in the blink of an eye. Whether it is shalom bayis, earning a livelihood, raising children—Hakadosh Baruch

וַיֵּרֶד מִצְרַיְמָה. אָנוּס עַל פִּי הַדִּבּוּר.

וַיָּגָר שָׁם. מְלַמֵּד שֶׁלֹּא יָרַד יַעֲקֹב אָבִינוּ לְהִשְׁתַּקֵּעַ בְּמִצְרַיִם, אֶלָּא לָגוּר שָׁם, שֶׁנֶּאֱמַר: וַיֹּאמְרוּ אֶל פַּרְעֹה, לָגוּר בָּאָרֶץ בָּאנוּ, כִּי אֵין מִרְעֶה לַצֹּאן אֲשֶׁר לַעֲבָדֶיךָ, כִּי כָבֵד הָרָעָב בְּאֶרֶץ כְּנָעַן. וְעַתָּה, יֵשְׁבוּ נָא עֲבָדֶיךָ בְּאֶרֶץ גֹּשֶׁן:

בִּמְתֵי מְעָט. כְּמָה שֶׁנֶּאֱמַר: בְּשִׁבְעִים נֶפֶשׁ, יָרְדוּ אֲבֹתֶיךָ מִצְרָיְמָה. וְעַתָּה, שָׂמְךָ יְיָ אֱלֹהֶיךָ, כְּכוֹכְבֵי הַשָּׁמַיִם לָרֹב.

וַיְהִי שָׁם לְגוֹי. מְלַמֵּד שֶׁהָיוּ יִשְׂרָאֵל מְצֻיָּנִים שָׁם:

פירוש

Hu can deliver us out of the most difficult situations in wondrous, miraculous ways.

♦ ♦ ♦ ♦ ♦ ♦

What is it that has sustained the Jews while countless other nations have faded into history? It appears from the Haggadah that Hakadosh Boruch Hu's ever-present protection has allowed us to endure. However, there are two things that serve as conduits for that protection.

First and foremost, of course, is the Torah. We are told (Deut. 4:4), "ואתם הדבקים בה' אלוקיכם חיים כלכם היום—You who cleave to Hashem, your G-d, all of you are living today." Torah is life. When the overwhelming majority of Jews live a Torah life, retain their traditions, and remain insulated from the prevailing culture, they are blessed with life.

If, G-d forbid, we assimilate, and neglect the Torah, there is another guarantee of our survival—our enemies' hatred of us. "הלכה היא בידוע שעשו שונא ליעקב—It is a halacha that Eisav hates Yaakov." This is no mere theory or philosophy; it is a halacha—an absolute rule. When we choose to join the nations that surround us, when we forgo Torah in favor of worldly culture, chas v'shalom, the very people we wish to join will per

"*And he went down to Egypt*"—compelled by the divine decree.

"*And he sojourned there*"—This teaches us that he did not go down to settle in Egypt but only to sojourn there. As it is stated, "And Jacob's sons said to Pharaoh, 'We have come to sojourn in the land, for your servants' flocks have no pasture, for the famine is severe in the land of Canaan. Now, please let your servants dwell in the land of Goshen" (Bereishis 47:4).

"*Few in number*"—as it is stated, "With seventy souls your fathers went down to Egypt. Now Hashem, your God has made you like the stars of heaven for multitude" (Devarim 10:22).

"*And there he became a great nation*"—This teaches us that Israel was distinguished there.

◆ פירוש ◆

secute us. This is the key to survival. And this is what has sustained us.

The Haggadah teaches us that "בכל דור ודור עומדים עלינו לכלותינו—In every generation, the nations of the world stand up against us." They persecute us. And this persecution is our salvation.

Our enemies continually remind us of our Jewishness. They don't let us forget. They cry out to us: "Remember, you are a Jew! Don't forget, you are a Jew!"

This constant reminder of our Jewishness combined with Divine protection has sustained us. But "הקב"ה מצילנו מידם—Hakadosh Baruch Hu saves us from their hands."

◆ ◆ ◆ ◆ ◆ ◆

One of the first challenges Klal Yisroel faced occurred immediately following *kriyas Yam Suf*, notes HaGaon HaRav Simcha Wasserman zt"l. The Torah (Shemos 15) says, "וילכו שלשת ימים במדבר ולא מצאו מים—And they traveled three days in the desert, and they didn't find water." We are taught, "הוי כל צמא לכו למים—Let all who are thirsty go to the water." Meforshim say that water refers to Torah—"אין מים אלא תורה."

When the Jews complained of thirst, the prophets in their midst

גָּדוֹל עָצוּם. כְּמָה שֶׁנֶּאֱמַר: וּבְנֵי יִשְׂרָאֵל, פָּרוּ וַיִּשְׁרְצוּ, וַיִּרְבּוּ וַיַּעַצְמוּ, בִּמְאֹד מְאֹד, וַתִּמָּלֵא הָאָרֶץ אֹתָם:

וָרָב. כְּמָה שֶׁנֶּאֱמַר: רְבָבָה כְּצֶמַח הַשָּׂדֶה נְתַתִּיךְ, וַתִּרְבִּי, וַתִּגְדְּלִי, וַתָּבֹאִי בַּעֲדִי עֲדָיִים: שָׁדַיִם נָכֹנוּ, וּשְׂעָרֵךְ צִמֵּחַ, וְאַתְּ עֵרֹם וְעֶרְיָה: וָאֶעֱבֹר עָלַיִךְ וָאֶרְאֵךְ מִתְבּוֹסֶסֶת בְּדָמָיִךְ, וָאֹמַר לָךְ, בְּדָמַיִךְ חֲיִי, וָאֹמַר לָךְ, בְּדָמַיִךְ חֲיִי.

וַיָּרֵעוּ אֹתָנוּ הַמִּצְרִים וַיְעַנּוּנוּ. וַיִּתְּנוּ עָלֵינוּ עֲבֹדָה קָשָׁה:

וַיָּרֵעוּ אֹתָנוּ הַמִּצְרִים. כְּמָה שֶׁנֶּאֱמַר: הָבָה נִתְחַכְּמָה לוֹ. פֶּן יִרְבֶּה, וְהָיָה כִּי תִקְרֶאנָה מִלְחָמָה, וְנוֹסַף גַּם הוּא עַל שֹׂנְאֵינוּ, וְנִלְחַם בָּנוּ וְעָלָה מִן הָאָרֶץ:

♦ פירוש ♦

immediately deduced that they suffered from a lack of Torah. It was then that they instituted the *takkanah* that the Torah should be read on Shabbos, Monday, and Thursday. This guaranteed that no Jewish man would find himself without Torah for three consecutive days.

But the timing of this new ruling should give us pause. Was this the first time Klal Yisroel was without Torah for three days? What about the week between *yetzias* Mitzrayim and *kriyas Yam Suf*? And what about the two hundred and ten years the Jews were in galus in Mitzrayim? They didn't learn Torah then. Why was there no need to institute such a program before? How did the Jewish nation survive?

The answer is that the Jews were persecuted! For two hundred and ten years, the Egyptians tortured the Jews. The Jews couldn't forget who they were, because their overseers didn't let them forget. Even after *yetzias* Mitzrayim, they could not forget; their pursuers reminded them.

But after they witnessed their tormentors drown in the sea, there was

"Strong"—as it is stated, "The children of Israel were fruitful and swarmed and increased and became very very strong, and the land became filled with them" (Shemos 1:7).

"Numerous"—as it is stated, "Myriads, like the plants of the field I have made you, and you have increased and grown, and you come with perfect beauty, breasts fashioned and your hair grown, but you were naked and bare" (Yechezkel 16:7). And I passed over you and saw you downtrodden in your blood and I said to you: 'Through your blood you shall live!' And I said to you: 'Through your blood shall you live!'

"And the Egyptians mistreated us and afflicted us and imposed hard labor upon us" (Devarim 26:6).

"And the Egyptians mistreated us"—as it is stated, "Come, let us deal shrewdly with them, lest they increase, and if a war befalls us, they will join our enemies and fight against us and leave the land" (Shemos 1:10).

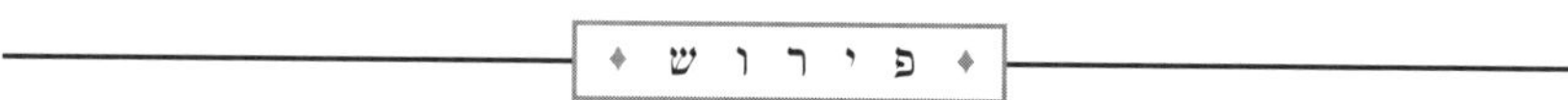

no longer something to ensure their survival. They needed Torah to survive, as do we.

♦ ♦ ♦ ♦ ♦ ♦

When Rabbi Yecheskel Levenstein, the famed mashgiach of the Mir Yeshiva in the late 1930's, fell ill, he was taken to a hospital where doctors talked about the possible need for a blood transfusion. Rabbi Levenstein became upset.

"I have been praying all my life not to need מתנת בשר ודם (the gift of flesh and blood, generally interpreted as 'gifts from a human being'). Will I really have to accept blood from a human being now?"

"Is that the simple meaning of the phrase מתנת בשר ודם?" asked a talmid.

וַיְעַנּוּנוּ. כְּמָה שֶׁנֶּאֱמַר: וַיָּשִׂימוּ עָלָיו שָׂרֵי מִסִּים, לְמַעַן עַנֹּתוֹ בְּסִבְלֹתָם: וַיִּבֶן עָרֵי מִסְכְּנוֹת לְפַרְעֹה, אֶת פִּתֹם וְאֶת רַעַמְסֵס: וַיִּתְּנוּ עָלֵינוּ עֲבֹדָה קָשָׁה. כְּמָה שֶׁנֶּאֱמַר: וַיַּעֲבִדוּ מִצְרַיִם אֶת בְּנֵי יִשְׂרָאֵל בְּפָרֶךְ:

◆ פירוש ◆

Rabbi Levenstein answered: "The influence of a prayer in heaven goes as far as the thought one has invested it with on earth. If we pray with a specific interpretation of the words in mind, we can bring about the blessings we have intended through our *kavanos* (thoughts)."

◆ ◆ ◆ ◆ ◆ ◆

Jews have always struggled, always been persecuted. But throughout history, we have retained our Jewishness, in spite of, or as Rav Wasserman teaches, because of the persecution.

The concentration camp Theresienstadt was no different. Here Jews were persecuted, here they had to live, here they died because they were Jews. There was only one difference. Theresienstadt played a key role in the Nazi propaganda war. Jews were persecuted there, as they were in camps scattered throughout Eastern Europe, but the persecution was not always obvious.

When Red Cross representatives visited the camp, the inmates were ordered to pretend. They pretended to study, they pretended to play, and they knew that any indication to the guests that things were not quite right would cost them their lives.

However, most of them lost their lives anyway. There were 15,000 children in Theresienstadt. Only 100 returned from the place the train tracks led to. You wouldn't think there was time or passion left for poem writing. But they wrote, and they drew. And though these 14,900 children are lost forever, their writings and drawings live on.

I know, because when I visited Theresienstadt, better known as Terezin, in Bohemia (what is now the Czech Republic), I saw those writings and drawings. One poem in particular struck me. The indomitable Jewish spirit of the 14-year-old poet lives on; it is a spirit that persecution

"*And afflicted us*"—as it is stated, "They appointed over them taskmasters to afflict them with their burdens, and they built store cities for Pharaoh; Pithom and Raamses" (Shemos 1:11). "And imposed hard labor upon us"—as it is stated, "The Egyptians enslaved the children of Israel with back-breaking labor" (Shemos 1:13).

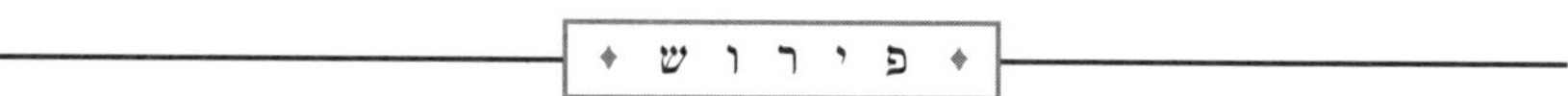

could not quell.

I am a Jew

I am a Jew, a Jew I shall remain,
Even if I die of hunger
I will not give up my nation,
I will fight always
For my nation, on my honor.
I will never be ashamed
Of my nation, on my honor.

I am proud of my nation,
A nation most worthy of honor.
I shall always be oppressed,
I shall always live again. *F. Bass (1943)*

♦ ♦ ♦ ♦ ♦ ♦

עֲבֹדָה קָשָׁה

Chazal tell us that what was so difficult about the work in Egypt was that the Egyptians forced the women to do work suited for men, and the men, to do work suited for women. We can understand why this was hard on the women, who were forced to do heavy manual labor. But why was it so difficult for the men?

Men and women have different roles in life. And they are equipped with the natures to fill them. It can be difficult to ask a woman to do the work of a man, or a man the work of a woman, because they do not have the inherent tools to do the job.

וַנִּצְעַק אֶל יְיָ אֱלֹהֵי אֲבֹתֵינוּ, וַיִּשְׁמַע יְיָ אֶת קֹלֵנוּ, וַיַּרְא אֶת עָנְיֵנוּ, וְאֶת עֲמָלֵנוּ, וְאֶת לַחֲצֵנוּ:

וַנִּצְעַק אֶל יְיָ אֱלֹהֵי אֲבֹתֵינוּ. כְּמָה שֶׁנֶּאֱמַר: וַיְהִי בַיָּמִים הָרַבִּים הָהֵם, וַיָּמָת מֶלֶךְ מִצְרַיִם, וַיֵּאָנְחוּ בְנֵי יִשְׂרָאֵל מִן הָעֲבֹדָה וַיִּזְעָקוּ. וַתַּעַל שַׁוְעָתָם אֶל הָאֱלֹהִים מִן הָעֲבֹדָה:

וַיִּשְׁמַע יְיָ אֶת קֹלֵנוּ. כְּמָה שֶׁנֶּאֱמַר: וַיִּשְׁמַע אֱלֹהִים אֶת נַאֲקָתָם, וַיִּזְכֹּר אֱלֹהִים אֶת בְּרִיתוֹ, אֶת אַבְרָהָם, אֶת יִצְחָק, וְאֶת יַעֲקֹב:

♦ פירוש ♦

A woman has special kochos to raise children, and instill in them emunah, yiras shomayim, and a love of chesed. The role of *akeres habayis* is much more than "housewife." A woman is the foundation of the home.

A man sets the tone and the ruach for the family to emulate through his avodas Hashem and limud Torah.

Harmony in the home is best achieved when both men and women each fulfill their unique roles, as they contribute to the building of their mikdash me'at (miniature Sanctuary).

An example of how men must instill Torah values in their children can be illustrated with the following story: A man brought his son to Rabbi Yecheskel Levenstein for a bracha. He asked that the mashgiach bless his son to grow up to be a *masmid*, to be diligent in his Torah studies. Rabbi Levenstein responded by turning to the father and asking him:

"Do you learn diligently?"

The father lowered his eyes. "I don't have time to learn," he admitted.

"If you want your son to become a *masmid*," answered the mashgiach, "you must first become one yourself. Your son will follow in your footsteps."

"And we cried out to Hashem, the God of our fathers, and Hashem heard our voice and saw our affliction, our toil, and our oppression" (Devarim 26:7).

"And we cried out to Hashem, the God of our fathers"—as it is stated, "It came to pass in those many days that the king of Egypt died, and the children of Israel sighed from the labor, and they cried out, and their cry ascended to God from the labor" (Shemos 2:23).

"And Hashem heard our voice"—as it is stated, "God heard their cry, and God remembered His covenant with Abraham, with Isaac, and with Jacob" (Shemos 2:24).

♦ פ י ר ו ש ♦

הָבָה נִתְחַכְּמָה לוֹ

The Egyptians wanted to impress the Jews with their wisdom. Their intention was to persuade the Jews to assimilate, learn Egyptian ways, and accept their culture.

Similarly, today we are lured to accumulate the knowledge of our surrounding culture, often at dangerous risk to our spirituality. Indeed, we must be especially wary of where we choose to educate our children.

Rabbi Nosson Tzvi Finkel, the Alter of Slabodka, once passed the center of town in the 1920's in Lithuania. Shocked at the moral depravity and emptiness, he was heartbroken. It took a while for him to recover.

What should *we* say? Imagine how he would react today!

♦ ♦ ♦ ♦ ♦ ♦

וְאֶת עֲמָלֵנוּ. אֵלּוּ הַבָּנִים

When we are blessed with children, we should remember the words "ואת עמלנו אלו הבנים—and our hard work, these are the children." Having children is a blessing as well as an obligation. Parents are obligated to work diligently on their children's chinuch. Each precious child must be raised with sensitivity and effort.

וַיַּרְא אֶת עָנְיֵנוּ. זוֹ פְּרִישׁוּת דֶּרֶךְ אֶרֶץ. כְּמָה שֶּׁנֶּאֱמַר: וַיַּרְא אֱלֹהִים אֶת בְּנֵי יִשְׂרָאֵל. וַיֵּדַע אֱלֹהִים:

וְאֶת עֲמָלֵנוּ. אֵלּוּ הַבָּנִים. כְּמָה שֶּׁנֶּאֱמַר: כָּל הַבֵּן הַיִּלּוֹד הַיְאֹרָה תַּשְׁלִיכֻהוּ, וְכָל הַבַּת תְּחַיּוּן:

וְאֶת לַחֲצֵנוּ. זֶה הַדְּחַק. כְּמָה שֶּׁנֶּאֱמַר: וְגַם רָאִיתִי אֶת הַלַּחַץ, אֲשֶׁר מִצְרַיִם לֹחֲצִים אֹתָם:

וַיּוֹצִאֵנוּ יְיָ מִמִּצְרַיִם, בְּיָד חֲזָקָה, וּבִזְרֹעַ נְטוּיָה, וּבְמֹרָא גָּדוֹל וּבְאֹתוֹת וּבְמוֹפְתִים:

וַיּוֹצִאֵנוּ יְיָ מִמִּצְרַיִם. לֹא עַל יְדֵי מַלְאָךְ, וְלֹא עַל יְדֵי שָׂרָף. וְלֹא עַל יְדֵי שָׁלִיחַ. אֶלָּא הַקָּדוֹשׁ בָּרוּךְ הוּא בִּכְבוֹדוֹ וּבְעַצְמוֹ. שֶׁנֶּאֱמַר: וְעָבַרְתִּי בְאֶרֶץ מִצְרַיִם בַּלַּיְלָה הַזֶּה, וְהִכֵּיתִי כָל בְּכוֹר בְּאֶרֶץ מִצְרַיִם, מֵאָדָם וְעַד בְּהֵמָה, וּבְכָל אֱלֹהֵי מִצְרַיִם אֶעֱשֶׂה שְׁפָטִים אֲנִי יְיָ:

פירוש

Every Jew is obligated in chinuch, says the great 19th century cha sidic Rabbi, Rabbi Sholom Dov Ber, known as the Rashab. There is no difference between a talmid chochom and the simple Jewish man with regard to wearing tefillin, and there is no difference between them with regard to chinuch. Both tefillin and chinuch must be done daily, without exception, by each and every Jewish male.

A parent is obligated to spend at least a half hour each day, contem plating his children's education, and planning for their success. He must invest all of his strengths, and even go beyond his strengths, to teach his children to tread the proper path.

"And he saw our affliction"—This refers to the separation of a man from his wife, as it is stated, "And God saw the children of Israel, and God knew" (Shemos 2:24).

"Our toil"—This refers to the sons, as it is stated, "Every son who is born you shall cast into the Nile, and every daughter you shall allow to live" (Shemos 1:22).

"And our oppression"—This refers to the pressure of their hard work, as it is stated, "and I have also seen the oppression that the Egyptians are oppressing them" (Shemos 3:9).

"And Hashem took us out of Egypt with a mighty hand, and with an outstretched arm, and with a great revelation, and with signs and wonders" (Devarim 26:8).

"And Hashem took us out of Egypt"—not by the hand of an angel, not by the hand of a seraph, not by the hand of a messenger, but by the Holy One blessed is He, in His Glory, Himself, as it is stated, "I will pass through the land of Egypt on this night, and I will strike every firstborn in the land of Egypt, both man and beast, and upon all the gods of Egypt will I wreak judgments—I, Hashem" (Shemos 12:12).

אֲנִי וְלֹא מַלְאָךְ

Rabbi Yehuda Sofer in his sefer, *Peninei HaGeulah,* comments that not only would it have been impossible for the *malochim* to redeem the Jews, but if they would have descended into Egypt, they themselves would have been immediately destroyed by the impurity of the atmosphere. It was Hashem's Essence alone that could descend into such impurity and still bring about Bnai Yisroel's redemption.

Rav Eliyahu Dessler comments that just as there are physical germs which are contagious and can be transmitted, so too there are germs on a spiritual level which are contagious and can contaminate. Therefore, the

וְעָבַרְתִּי בְאֶרֶץ מִצְרַיִם בַּלַּיְלָה הַזֶּה, אֲנִי וְלֹא מַלְאָךְ. וְהִכֵּיתִי כָל בְּכוֹר בְּאֶרֶץ מִצְרַיִם. אֲנִי וְלֹא שָׂרָף. וּבְכָל אֱלֹהֵי מִצְרַיִם אֶעֱשֶׂה שְׁפָטִים, אֲנִי וְלֹא הַשָּׁלִיחַ. אֲנִי יְיָ. אֲנִי הוּא וְלֹא אַחֵר:

בְּיָד חֲזָקָה. זוֹ הַדֶּבֶר. כְּמָה שֶׁנֶּאֱמַר: הִנֵּה יַד יְיָ הוֹיָה, בְּמִקְנְךָ אֲשֶׁר בַּשָּׂדֶה, בַּסּוּסִים בַּחֲמֹרִים בַּגְּמַלִּים, בַּבָּקָר וּבַצֹּאן, דֶּבֶר כָּבֵד מְאֹד:

וּבִזְרֹעַ נְטוּיָה. זוֹ הַחֶרֶב. כְּמָה שֶׁנֶּאֱמַר: וְחַרְבּוֹ שְׁלוּפָה בְּיָדוֹ, נְטוּיָה עַל יְרוּשָׁלָיִם:

וּבְמוֹרָא גָּדוֹל. זוֹ גִּלּוּי שְׁכִינָה. כְּמָה שֶׁנֶּאֱמַר: אוֹ הֲנִסָּה אֱלֹהִים, לָבוֹא לָקַחַת לוֹ גוֹי מִקֶּרֶב גּוֹי, בְּמַסֹּת בְּאֹתֹת וּבְמוֹפְתִים וּבְמִלְחָמָה, וּבְיָד חֲזָקָה וּבִזְרוֹעַ נְטוּיָה, וּבְמוֹרָאִים גְּדֹלִים. כְּכֹל אֲשֶׁר עָשָׂה לָכֶם יְיָ אֱלֹהֵיכֶם בְּמִצְרַיִם, לְעֵינֶיךָ:

וּבְאֹתוֹת. זֶה הַמַּטֶּה, כְּמָה שֶׁנֶּאֱמַר: וְאֶת הַמַּטֶּה הַזֶּה תִּקַּח בְּיָדֶךָ. אֲשֶׁר תַּעֲשֶׂה בּוֹ אֶת הָאֹתֹת:

פ י ר ו ש

words of the Mishnah in Avos (1:7) "הרחק משכן רע—to distance ourselves from a bad neighbor" is to be taken quite literally. Even entering into close proximity of evil presents an enormous danger.

◆ ◆ ◆ ◆ ◆ ◆

וּבְאֹתוֹת. זֶה הַמַּטֶּה

Rabbi Shmuel Borenstein of Sochotchov writes in his sefer *Shem*

"I will pass through the land of Egypt on this night"—I, and not an angel. "And I will strike every firstborn in the land of Egypt"—I, and not a seraph. "And upon all the gods of Egypt will I wreak judgments"—I, and not a messenger. "I, Hashem"—it is I and not another.

"*With a mighty hand*"—This refers to the pestilence, as it is stated, "Behold, the hand of Hashem will be upon your livestock that is in the field, upon the horses, upon the donkeys, upon the camels, upon the cattle, and upon the sheep; a very severe pestilence" (Shemos 9:3).

"*And with an outstretched arm*"—This refers to the sword, as it is stated, "And a drawn sword in his hand, outstretched over Jerusalem" (Divrei Hayamim I, 21:16).

"*And with a great revelation*"—This refers to the revelation of God's presence, as it is stated, "Or has God proven Himself to come, to take a nation from the midst of another nation, with demonstrations of power, with signs and with wonders, and with war, and with a mighty hand and an outstretched arm, and with great revelations, like all that Hashem, your God, did for you in Egypt before your eyes" (Devarim 4:34).

"*With signs*"—This refers to the staff, as it is stated, "And you shall take this staff in your hand with which to perform the signs" (Yoel 3:3).

M'Shmuel that in Pirkei Avos (5:6), we see that Moshe Rabbeinu's staff was created on the evening of the sixth day, during the period when the sun had begun to set (*bein hashmashos*).

Actually, the staff first belonged to Yaakov Avinu. Yaakov used the staff to split and pass through the Jordan River. Moshe Rabbeinu used it to perform a multitude of miracles, and to prove the miracles of creation.

But the most extraordinary miracles the staff will perform will be at the hands of Moshiach. Then, Hashem will send the staff from Zion,

וּבְמוֹפְתִים. זֶה הַדָּם. כְּמָה שֶׁנֶּאֱמַר: וְנָתַתִּי מוֹפְתִים, בַּשָּׁמַיִם וּבָאָרֶץ:

At the mention of each of the following three wonders—blood, fire, and pillars of smoke—we dip a finger into our wine cup and remove a drop of wine.

דָּם. וָאֵשׁ. וְתִימְרוֹת עָשָׁן:

דָּבָר אַחֵר. בְּיָד חֲזָקָה שְׁתַּיִם. וּבִזְרֹעַ נְטוּיָה שְׁתַּיִם. וּבְמוֹרָא גָּדוֹל שְׁתַּיִם. וּבְאֹתוֹת שְׁתַּיִם. וּבְמֹפְתִים שְׁתַּיִם: אֵלּוּ עֶשֶׂר מַכּוֹת שֶׁהֵבִיא הַקָּדוֹשׁ בָּרוּךְ הוּא עַל הַמִּצְרִים בְּמִצְרַיִם, וְאֵלּוּ הֵן:

At the mention of each of the following ten plagues, we dip a finger into our wine cup and remove a drop of wine.

דָּם. צְפַרְדֵּעַ. כִּנִּים. עָרוֹב. דֶּבֶר. שְׁחִין. בָּרָד. אַרְבֶּה. חֹשֶׁךְ. מַכַּת בְּכוֹרוֹת:

רַבִּי יְהוּדָה הָיָה נוֹתֵן בָּהֶם סִמָּנִים:

At the mention of each of the abbreviations we dip a finger into our wine cup and remove a drop of wine. The cup is refilled afterwards.

דְּצַ״ךְ עֲדַ״שׁ בְּאַחַ״ב:

פירוש

where it will show the world His strength. "מטה עוזך ישלח ד׳ מציון—The staff of Your might, Hashem will send from Zion" (Tehillim 110:2).

◆ ◆ ◆ ◆ ◆ ◆

וּבְמוֹפְתִים. זֶה הַדָּם.

HaGaon HaRav Avigdor Miller zt"l, comments: Blood is life. It is the source of life, and the connecting force between body and soul. The Nile River was to Egypt what blood is to humans. It was the lifeblood of ancient Egypt, crucial to Egypt's agriculture and central to nearly every facet of Egypt's existence. It coursed through the country, irrigating crops

"*And with wonders*"—This refers to the blood, as it is stated, "And I will exhibit wonders in heaven and on earth—

At the mention of each of the following three wonders—blood, fire, and pillars of smoke—we dip a finger into our wine cup and remove a drop of wine.

Blood and fire and pillars of smoke."

Another explanation: "with a mighty hand" refers to two plagues, "and with an outstretched arm," another two, "and with a great revelation," another two, "and with signs," another two, "and with wonders," another two plagues. This refers to the ten plagues that the Holy One, blessed is He, brought upon the Egyptians in Egypt. They are:

At the mention of each of the following ten plagues, we dip a finger into our wine cup and remove a drop of wine.

Blood. Frogs. Lice. Wild beasts. Pestilence. Boils. Hail. Locusts. Darkness. Slaying of the firstborn.

Rabbi Judah abbreviated them, thus:

At the mention of each of the abbreviations we dip a finger into our wine cup and remove a drop of wine. The cup is refilled afterwards.

D'TZACH, ADASH, B'ACHAV

פירוש

and sustaining the people. In the first plague, by turning the Nile into blood, Hashem showed the Egyptians that the Nile, and all life, comes from Him, and that they are dependent upon Him for life itself.

♦ ♦ ♦ ♦ ♦ ♦

דָּם

By following the order of the plagues, we can learn how to lead our lives. Blood is warm, because it comes from the "foundation of fire." It is the opposite of the צפרדע (the frog), whose source is cold water.

Like the first *makkah*, blood, we must first take care of our "warmth,"

רַבִּי יוֹסֵי הַגְּלִילִי אוֹמֵר: מִנַּיִן אַתָּה אוֹמֵר, שֶׁלָּקוּ הַמִּצְרִים בְּמִצְרַיִם עֶשֶׂר מַכּוֹת, וְעַל הַיָּם, לָקוּ חֲמִשִּׁים מַכּוֹת? בְּמִצְרַיִם מָה הוּא אוֹמֵר: וַיֹּאמְרוּ הַחַרְטֻמִּם אֶל פַּרְעֹה, אֶצְבַּע אֱלֹהִים הִוא. וְעַל הַיָּם מָה הוּא אוֹמֵר? וַיַּרְא יִשְׂרָאֵל אֶת הַיָּד הַגְּדֹלָה, אֲשֶׁר עָשָׂה יְיָ בְּמִצְרַיִם, וַיִּירְאוּ הָעָם אֶת יְיָ. וַיַּאֲמִינוּ בַּייָ, וּבְמֹשֶׁה עַבְדּוֹ. כַּמָּה לָקוּ בְּאֶצְבַּע, עֶשֶׂר מַכּוֹת: אֱמוֹר מֵעַתָּה, בְּמִצְרַיִם לָקוּ עֶשֶׂר מַכּוֹת, וְעַל הַיָּם, לָקוּ חֲמִשִּׁים מַכּוֹת:

רַבִּי אֱלִיעֶזֶר אוֹמֵר: מִנַּיִן שֶׁכָּל מַכָּה וּמַכָּה, שֶׁהֵבִיא הַקָּדוֹשׁ בָּרוּךְ הוּא עַל הַמִּצְרִים בְּמִצְרַיִם, הָיְתָה שֶׁל אַרְבַּע מַכּוֹת? שֶׁנֶּאֱמַר: יְשַׁלַּח בָּם חֲרוֹן אַפּוֹ, עֶבְרָה וָזַעַם וְצָרָה. מִשְׁלַחַת מַלְאֲכֵי רָעִים. עֶבְרָה אַחַת. וָזַעַם שְׁתַּיִם. וְצָרָה שָׁלֹשׁ. מִשְׁלַחַת מַלְאֲכֵי רָעִים אַרְבַּע: אֱמוֹר מֵעַתָּה, בְּמִצְרַיִם לָקוּ אַרְבָּעִים מַכּוֹת, וְעַל הַיָּם לָקוּ מָאתַיִם מַכּוֹת:

פ י ר ו ש

meaning our spirituality. Only afterward can we focus on the "water," signifying our physical and material needs.

The power of warmth and spirituality can be illustrated by the following story:

A man once came to the Baal Shem Tov and begged the tzaddik to help him.

"I'm a natural thief," he admitted sadly. "I have tried but I absolutely cannot control my impulses. If I see something, I take it," he cried. "I want to stop! I must stop!"

The Baal Shem Tov invited the thief to join him in Torah study. Over a period of time he slowly influenced the man to raise his spiritual level. Later, the man recounted how the warmth of the Baal Shem Tov's Torah

Rabbi Yosé the Galilean said: "From where can we deduce that the Egyptians were stricken with ten plagues in Egypt, and with fifty plagues at sea? With regard to the plagues in Egypt, what is stated? 'And the magicians said to Pharaoh, "It is the finger of God" (Shemos 8:15). With regard to the plagues at the sea, what is stated? 'And Israel saw the great hand, which Hashem had used upon the Egyptians, and the people feared God, and they believed in God and in Moses, his servant" (Shemos 14:31). How many plagues did they receive by one finger? Ten plagues. Thus it follows—in Egypt they were dealt ten plagues, and at the sea they were dealt fifty plagues.

Rabbi Eliezer said: "From where can we deduce that each plague the Holy One, blessed is He, brought upon the Egyptians in Egypt consisted of four plagues? As it is stated, 'He dispatched against them the kindling of His anger—wrath, fury, and trouble, a delegation of evil messengers.' 'Wrath' indicates one plague; 'fury,' two; 'trouble,' three; 'a delegation of evil messengers,' four. Thus it follows—in Egypt they were dealt forty plagues, and at sea they were dealt two hundred plagues."

made it unthinkable for him to continue his corrupt way of life.

♦ ♦ ♦ ♦ ♦ ♦

Why were the Egyptians smitten with the plague of blood?

When Hevel murdered his brother Kayin, Hashem reproached him, saying, "The voice of your brother's blood is crying out to you." Ever since then, the blood of the murdered refuses to be stilled. It shouts out to the heavens, accusing the murderer.

With the advent of the plague of blood, the Egyptians were faced with their murders. They sensed that the blood in the Nile was the blood of the innocent children they had flung into its waters. The blood screamed out to the Heavens, accusing the Egyptians for their wrongful

רַבִּי עֲקִיבָא אוֹמֵר: מִנַּיִן שֶׁכָּל מַכָּה וּמַכָּה, שֶׁהֵבִיא הַקָּדוֹשׁ בָּרוּךְ הוּא עַל הַמִּצְרִים בְּמִצְרַיִם, הָיְתָה שֶׁל חָמֵשׁ מַכּוֹת? שֶׁנֶּאֱמַר: יְשַׁלַּח בָּם חֲרוֹן אַפּוֹ, עֶבְרָה וָזַעַם וְצָרָה. מִשְׁלַחַת מַלְאֲכֵי רָעִים. חֲרוֹן אַפּוֹ אַחַת. עֶבְרָה שְׁתַּיִם. וָזַעַם שָׁלֹשׁ. וְצָרָה אַרְבַּע. מִשְׁלַחַת מַלְאֲכֵי רָעִים חָמֵשׁ: אֱמוֹר מֵעַתָּה, בְּמִצְרַיִם לָקוּ חֲמִשִּׁים מַכּוֹת, וְעַל הַיָּם לָקוּ חֲמִשִּׁים וּמָאתַיִם מַכּוֹת:

פירוש

death. For the first time, the Egyptians were forced to confront their murderous deeds.

"וניקתי דמם לא ניקתי ה׳ שוכן בציון—Though I cleanse [the enemy] their bloodshed I will not cleanse" (Yoel 4:21). ציון has the same gematriya as קנאה (avenge). When the Shechinah is in Tzion then our enemies will be avenged.

♦ ♦ ♦ ♦ ♦ ♦

צְפַרְדֵּעַ

The word צפרדע is built of the word צפיר, meaning morning, and דע, meaning to know. The frogs knew to croak and cry all night in order to disturb the Egyptians sleep. When morning came, they knew it was time to stop.

We live in times when we already feel the stirrings of the era of Moshiach. We, too, should emulate the frogs and cry all night—we should become involved in teshuva and prayer. When Moshiach will arrive, a new dawn will break upon the world, and, like the frogs, we will rejoice that we have cried during the night of galus.

♦ ♦ ♦ ♦ ♦ ♦

אַרְבֶּה

In 1959, Eretz Yisroel was smitten with a locust swarm. A cloud of

Rabbi Akiva said: "From where can we deduce that each plague the Holy One, blessed is He, brought upon the Egyptians in Egypt consisted of five plagues? As it is stated, 'He sent forth against them the kindling of His anger—wrath, fury, and trouble, a delegation of evil messengers' (Tehillim 78:49). 'The kindling of His anger' indicates one plague; 'wrath,' two; 'fury,' three; 'trouble,' four; 'a delegation of evil messengers,' five. Thus it follows—in Egypt they were dealt fifty plagues, and at sea they were dealt two hundred and fifty plagues."

◆ פ י ר ו ש ◆

locusts swarmed upon farms, destroying crops and leaving a trail of devastation. Some farms, however, were spared. Those who had observed shmitah were untouched by the plague.

When the Rabbi of Brisk heard of the miracle, he said it should be widely publicized, because the Torah tells us about *makkas arbeh*, למען תספר באזני בנך—meaning you should recount miracles to your children. The Klausenberger Rebbe disagreed. He said the miracle should be kept secret to protect the farms from an evil eye. So we see that two gedolei hador continued to dispute the age-old question of how much of our blessings should be revealed and how much should remain private. Perhaps the notion that it's good to recount but not gloat, synthesizes both schools of thought.

◆ ◆ ◆ ◆ ◆ ◆

חֹשֶׁךְ

The Torah describes the plague of darkness: "A man did not see his brother, and a man did not get up from his place."

The Sfas Emes says that when "a man does not see his brother"—meaning, when each person is self-centered and cannot sense the needs of others, it will be impossible to transcend.

◆ ◆ ◆ ◆ ◆ ◆

כַּמָּה מַעֲלוֹת טוֹבוֹת לַמָּקוֹם עָלֵינוּ:

אִלּוּ הוֹצִיאָנוּ מִמִּצְרַיִם, וְלֹא עָשָׂה בָהֶם שְׁפָטִים, דַּיֵּנוּ:

אִלּוּ עָשָׂה בָהֶם שְׁפָטִים, וְלֹא עָשָׂה בֵאלֹהֵיהֶם, דַּיֵּנוּ:

אִלּוּ עָשָׂה בֵאלֹהֵיהֶם, וְלֹא הָרַג אֶת בְּכוֹרֵיהֶם, דַּיֵּנוּ:

אִלּוּ הָרַג אֶת בְּכוֹרֵיהֶם, וְלֹא נָתַן לָנוּ אֶת מָמוֹנָם, דַּיֵּנוּ:

אִלּוּ נָתַן לָנוּ אֶת מָמוֹנָם, וְלֹא קָרַע לָנוּ אֶת הַיָּם, דַּיֵּנוּ:

פירוש

One man who tried to always take care of other's needs was the Skulener Rebbe, HaGaon HaRav Eliezer Zisha Portugal zt"l, one of the well-known chasidic leaders of our time. One night, a man whose mother was in the hospital called the Skulener Rebbe. He asked the Rebbe to daven for his mother. The next evening, the Skulener's Rebbetzin called the man to find out if there had been any improvement in his mother's condition.

The man replied, "Why, yes! In fact, early this morning, around 5:00 a.m., her condition stabilized and they moved her from the intensive care unit to a regular room."

The Rebbetzin exclaimed, "You should've called the Rebbe! He has been davening and crying for her since your call last night!"

There is nothing quite so life-giving as helping another. Living for oneself is not life; it is death.

◆ ◆ ◆ ◆ ◆ ◆

וַיַּרְא יִשְׂרָאֵל אֶת הַיָּד הַגְּדֹלָה

HaGaon HaRav Avigdor Miller zt"l, comments that there are two types of sight. There is the vision we physically see with our eyes, and there is the vision which we see with our mind. Eyesight alone cannot raise one's level of emunah. In order to increase emunah, we must internalize what

How many favors has the Ever-Present bestowed upon us!

Had He brought us out of Egypt, but had not executed judg ment upon the Egyptians, it would have been sufficient for us.

Had He executed judgment upon them, but not upon their gods, it would been sufficient for us.

Had He executed judgment upon their gods, but had not slain their firstborn, it would have been sufficient for us.

Had He slain their firstborn, but had not given us their wealth, it would have been sufficient for us.

Had He given us their wealth, but had not split the sea for us, it would have been sufficient for us.

♦ פירוש ♦

our eyes have witnessed. We must begin to *see* with our minds. We must also take the time to think about the significance of what we have seen. Only then can it make an impression on us, transform our outlook, and bring us to greater heights in emunah.

The Jews at the *Yam Suf* saw "the great hand" of Hashem. The word יד, hand, implies that they understood that nothing was coincidental. They did not merely *see* the miracles; they internalized the miracles, and recognized that all that they had witnessed was from Hashem.

♦ ♦ ♦ ♦ ♦ ♦

וַיַּאֲמִינוּ בַּה׳, וּבְמֹשֶׁה עַבְדּוֹ

Even after the Jews witnessed the miracles of *kriyas Yam Suf* and the destruction of the Egyptian army, they needed emunah. They needed faith to sustain them through the passage of time. They needed faith that the spiritual impact of the moment, and the awakening they had experi enced, would not dwindle over time, but that they would remain forever strengthened by all that they had seen.

Often in life, we encounter the supernatural. We may be delivered from a near-death experience, receive an incredible blessing, or witness a breathtaking occurrence. At first, we may feel profoundly indebted to Hashem, Who has allowed us the privilege of taking part in the

אִלּוּ קָרַע לָנוּ אֶת הַיָּם, וְלֹא הֶעֱבִירָנוּ בְתוֹכוֹ בֶּחָרָבָה, דַּיֵּנוּ:

אִלּוּ הֶעֱבִירָנוּ בְתוֹכוֹ בֶּחָרָבָה, וְלֹא שִׁקַּע צָרֵינוּ בְּתוֹכוֹ, דַּיֵּנוּ:

אִלּוּ שִׁקַּע צָרֵינוּ בְּתוֹכוֹ,
וְלֹא סִפֵּק צָרְכֵּנוּ בַּמִּדְבָּר אַרְבָּעִים שָׁנָה, דַּיֵּנוּ:

אִלּוּ סִפֵּק צָרְכֵּנוּ בַּמִּדְבָּר אַרְבָּעִים שָׁנָה,
וְלֹא הֶאֱכִילָנוּ אֶת הַמָּן, דַּיֵּנוּ:

אִלּוּ הֶאֱכִילָנוּ אֶת הַמָּן, וְלֹא נָתַן לָנוּ אֶת הַשַּׁבָּת, דַּיֵּנוּ:

◆ פירוש ◆

miraculous.

However, all too often, our gratitude to Hashem will wane as the experience loses its newness, and as our daily routines overtake all our thoughts. It is vital that we remember the *chasdei* Hashem we have experienced, and maintain our emunah, and that long after life has returned to normal we continue to express our gratitude.

The Bobover Rebbe zt"l was someone who did not allow the passage of time to allow his *hakaras hatov* for Hashem's miracles to diminish. When the Rabbe was saved from the Nazis, he felt a tremendous debt of gratitude to Hashem for having spared him. Immediately, he vowed to celebrate a Melave Malka with his chassidim each Motzei Shabbos, to remember the miracles that Hashem performed for him. Each Seudas Melave Malka, for the rest of his life, was a celebration of gratitude, through which the Rebbe ensured that he would never cease to thank Hashem for having spared his life.

◆ ◆ ◆ ◆ ◆ ◆

HaGaon HaRav Eliezer Gordon zt"l from Telshe once commented: People think that secularists believe in nothing. This is false. They are believers but their belief is misguided. They don't believe in what we are

Had He split the sea for us, but had not led us through it on dry land, it would have been sufficient for us.

Had He led us through it on dry land, but had not drowned our oppressors in it, it would have been sufficient for us.

Had He drowned our oppressors in it, but had not provided for our needs in the desert for forty years, it would have been sufficient for us.

Had He provided for our needs in the desert for forty years, but had not fed us the manna, it would have been sufficient for us.

Had He fed us the manna, but had not given us Shabbos, it would have been sufficient for us.

obligated to believe in. Instead of believing in the true *neviim* (prophets), they believe in false prophets. The power of belief is found in every person; however, it's like all the other *kochos hanefesh* (a person's powers) that can either be used for righteous development and success, or can be abused and misdirected.

The power of belief is what sustained us over the generations, even in our darkest hour… The day that the Buchenwald concentration camp was liberated, an announcement was made over the loudspeaker that special Yom Tov services were going to be held later in the day in one of the bunkers, and everyone was invited to participate.

One of the survivors, a man named Moshe, wondered why, after all the horrors that his fellow inmates had experienced, anyone was even thinking about praying to Hashem! He himself certainly had no such plans. He was sure that few would show up to participate in the service. As the time approached, however, Moshe became extremely curious. He found himself edging towards the assigned meeting place to see what was going on. To his amazement, the entire room was packed with Jews who had come to express their thanks to Hashem for surviving. Witnessing this, Moshe was quite moved and said to himself, "Although a Jew's faith can be shaken, it is never lost."

אִלּוּ נָתַן לָנוּ אֶת הַשַּׁבָּת, וְלֹא קֵרְבָנוּ לִפְנֵי הַר סִינַי, דַּיֵּנוּ:

אִלּוּ קֵרְבָנוּ לִפְנֵי הַר סִינַי, וְלֹא נָתַן לָנוּ אֶת הַתּוֹרָה, דַּיֵּנוּ:

אִלּוּ נָתַן לָנוּ אֶת הַתּוֹרָה, וְלֹא הִכְנִיסָנוּ לְאֶרֶץ יִשְׂרָאֵל, דַּיֵּנוּ:

אִלּוּ הִכְנִיסָנוּ לְאֶרֶץ יִשְׂרָאֵל,
וְלֹא בָנָה לָנוּ אֶת בֵּית הַבְּחִירָה, דַּיֵּנוּ:

פ י ר ו ש

וְקָרַע לָנוּ אֶת הַיָּם

Chazal tell us, "מכאן קשה זווגו של אדם כקריעת ים סוף—a matrimonial match is as difficult as the splitting of the sea."

Why are shidduchim being compared to *kriyas Yam Suf*? What is the connection between them?

At the time of *kriyas Yam Suf*, the prosecuting angel (קטיגור) spoke up against Klal Yisroel. "הללו עובדי ע"ז והללו עובדי ע"ז—These [the Egyptians] serve idols, and these [the Jews] serve idols." The קטיגור was accusing Klal Yisroel of being unworthy of salvation!

The sea listened to this, but then, "הים ראה וינוס—the sea saw, and ran away." What did the sea see, and why did it run? It saw the Braisa of R' Yishmael, which instructs people what to do if they hear lashon hara: They should avoid listening to it by folding the soft part of their earlobe over the opening, to block out the sound.

When the *Yam* saw this Braisa, it realized that it had been listening to lashon hara about Bnei Yisrael, and therefore it fled to avoid hearing it—which resulted in the splitting of the sea (קריעת ים סוף). As the Chofetz Chaim explains, if it is impossible for us to avoid hearing loshon hora in the setting we are in, we should remove ourselves from the situation.

Like *kriyas Yam Suf*, shidduchim involve a lot of discussion about the various parties. There is often lashon hara spoken as people try to find out as much as they can before proceeding with a match. It can be difficult to strike the right balance between saying what should be said

Had He given us Shabbos, but had not brought us to Mount Sinai, it would have been sufficient for us.

Had He brought us to Mount Sinai, but had not given us the Torah, it would have been sufficient for us.

Had He given us the Torah, but had not brought us into the Land of Israel, it would have been sufficient for us.

Had He brought us into the Land of Israel, but had not built the Temple for us, it would have been sufficient for us.

while avoiding speaking lashon hara.

Just like the *Yam* ran, so too should we familiarize ourselves with the halachos of lashon hara and "run away" from any involvement with it (R' Yosef Poznovsky).

♦ ♦ ♦ ♦ ♦ ♦

R' Nachman of Breslov offers a profound insight into the challenge of guarding our tongue,

"When we are little we learn to talk. When we are old we learn to be quiet. That is one of the shortcomings of human beings; We learn to speak before we learn to be quiet."

♦ ♦ ♦ ♦ ♦ ♦

אִלּוּ נָתַן לָנוּ אֶת הַשַּׁבָּת, וְלֹא קֵרְבָנוּ לִפְנֵי הַר סִינַי

Shabbos observance brings Jews closer to Hashem and strengthens our emunah, says Rabbi Yisrael of Bohosh, who was an important chasidic Rebbe from the 1800's. That is why the Gemarah says that Shabbos is equal to all of the mitzvos (Yerushalmi 1:5).

Perhaps that is also why Chazal say that if all of Klal Yisroel would keep Shabbos only twice, they would all be redeemed. The observance of Shabbos by the entire nation would bring with it a resurgence in emunah. That faith, coupled with the merit of Shabbos, would be enough to bring about our redemption.

עַל אַחַת כַּמָּה וְכַמָּה טוֹבָה כְפוּלָה וּמְכֻפֶּלֶת לַמָּקוֹם עָלֵינוּ: שֶׁהוֹצִיאָנוּ מִמִּצְרַיִם, וְעָשָׂה בָהֶם שְׁפָטִים, וְעָשָׂה בֵאלֹהֵיהֶם, וְהָרַג אֶת בְּכוֹרֵיהֶם, וְנָתַן לָנוּ אֶת מָמוֹנָם, וְקָרַע לָנוּ אֶת הַיָּם, וְהֶעֱבִירָנוּ בְתוֹכוֹ בֶּחָרָבָה, וְשִׁקַּע צָרֵינוּ בְּתוֹכוֹ, וְסִפֵּק צָרְכֵּנוּ בַּמִּדְבָּר אַרְבָּעִים שָׁנָה, וְהֶאֱכִילָנוּ אֶת הַמָּן, וְנָתַן לָנוּ אֶת הַשַּׁבָּת, וְקֵרְבָנוּ לִפְנֵי הַר סִינַי, וְנָתַן לָנוּ אֶת הַתּוֹרָה, וְהִכְנִיסָנוּ לְאֶרֶץ יִשְׂרָאֵל, וּבָנָה לָנוּ אֶת בֵּית הַבְּחִירָה, לְכַפֵּר עַל כָּל עֲוֹנוֹתֵינוּ.

רַבָּן גַּמְלִיאֵל הָיָה אוֹמֵר: כָּל שֶׁלֹּא אָמַר שְׁלֹשָׁה דְבָרִים אֵלּוּ בַּפֶּסַח, לֹא יָצָא יְדֵי חוֹבָתוֹ, וְאֵלּוּ הֵן:

♦ פ י ר ו ש ♦

♦ ♦ ♦ ♦ ♦ ♦

When the Chofetz Chaim came to St. Petersburg for a rabbinical conference, a number of wealthy merchants came to the conference to meet and receive a blessing from the tzaddik. One man, who was not Shabbos observant, presented the Chofetz Chaim with a hefty donation for the yeshiva. The Chofetz Chaim grasped the man's arm.

"What a shame," he exclaimed. "Such a special hand that gives so much tzedakah is *mechalel* (disgraces) Shabbos."

The tzaddik grasped the man's hand and wept bitterly, gazing into the generous man's eyes, begging him to observe Shabbos. Shaken, the man, too, burst into tears. He vowed to make amends, and begin to observe Shabbos properly.

"There's just one thing I must ask," he said to the Chofetz Chaim. "There are several pressing matters I need to take care of this Shabbos. Give me one more week. After this week, I promise I'll keep every single Shabbos!"

The Chofetz Chaim grasped the man's hand once more. "My dear

How much more so are the favors, doubled and redoubled, that the Ever-Present has bestowed upon us!
He brought us out of Egypt, executed judgment upon them, executed judgment upon their gods, slew their firstborn, gave us their wealth, split the sea for us, led us through it on dry land, drowned our oppressors in it, provided for our needs in the desert for forty years, fed us the manna, gave us Shabbos, brought us to Mount Sinai, gave us the Torah, brought us into the Land of Israel, and built the Temple for us to atone for all our sins.

Rabban Gamliel used to say: "Whoever does not discuss these three things on Pesach has not fulfilled his obligation." And they are the following:

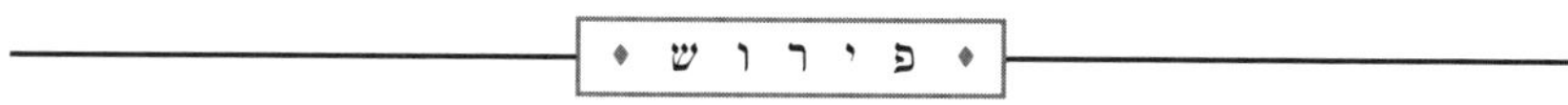

son," he said, "if the Shabbos were mine, I would tell you to take this one Shabbos, and finish up your affairs. But it's not mine—not mine at all. Shabbos belongs to Hashem. I cannot give you permission to work for even one moment of the holy day!"

The wealthy man was convinced. That week, he began his lifelong observance of Shabbos. (Hameoros HaGedolim)

♦ ♦ ♦ ♦ ♦ ♦

וּבָנָה לָנוּ אֶת בֵּית הַבְּחִירָה, לְכַפֵּר עַל כָּל עֲוֹנוֹתֵינוּ

The Beis Hamikdash was home to an abundance of holiness. There were the *korbanos*, the songs of the Leviim, the menorah, the *lechem hapanim;* the list is endless. And yet, the Baal Haggadah says that Hashem built the Beis Hamikdash to forgive our sins. Why is this ability to forgive mentioned, rather than the other special qualities of the Beis Hamikdash?

It is because teshuva is more powerful than everything else. Teshuva is so important, it reaches the Heavenly Throne. There is no human

פֶּסַח. מַצָּה וּמָרוֹר:

We gaze at, but do not lift, the shankbone and recite:

פֶּסַח שֶׁהָיוּ אֲבוֹתֵינוּ אוֹכְלִים, בִּזְמַן שֶׁבֵּית הַמִּקְדָּשׁ הָיָה קַיָּם, עַל שׁוּם מָה? עַל שׁוּם שֶׁפָּסַח הַקָּדוֹשׁ בָּרוּךְ הוּא, עַל בָּתֵּי אֲבוֹתֵינוּ בְּמִצְרַיִם, שֶׁנֶּאֱמַר: וַאֲמַרְתֶּם זֶבַח פֶּסַח הוּא לַייָ, אֲשֶׁר פָּסַח עַל בָּתֵּי בְנֵי יִשְׂרָאֵל בְּמִצְרַיִם, בְּנָגְפּוֹ אֶת מִצְרַיִם וְאֶת בָּתֵּינוּ הִצִּיל, וַיִּקֹּד הָעָם וַיִּשְׁתַּחֲווּ.

♦ פ י ר ו ש ♦

judge before whom a defendant can say, "I did the act you accuse me of, please forgive me." No judge would, or could, release such a person, but, unlike a human judge, Hashem only wants our sincere repentance.

Although we no longer have the Bais Hamikdash, we still have the power of teshuva and tefillah to change our lives. One day during the year when we all feel compelled to think about teshuva is Yom Kippur, however, it's possible that even Yom Kippur is taken for granted. Reb Yisroel Salanter reminds us that Yom Kippur is so precious that if we would have only a single day in our lifetime when our sins would be forgiven, we would be considered immensely fortunate! How fortunate we are that Hashem gives us this special day year after year!

♦ ♦ ♦ ♦ ♦ ♦

A discouraged chassid once visited Rabbi Avraham of Slonim. "I have been working on teshuva all my life," he said, "and I don't feel that I have become a better person. What will become of me?"

The tzaddik answered with a parable.

A traveler once found himself deep in a muddy swamp. He toiled and struggled, fighting to extricate himself from the morass and reach dry ground. Each step was identical to the one before—just one lift of his leg through the muck. But there was one difference. Each step brought him a bit nearer to the swamp's edge, and that much closer to freedom.

"You, too," said the Slonimer Rebbe, "feel as though you are lifting your leg in the effort for self improvement, only to discover that you are

the ***Pesach*** sacrifice, the ***unleavened bread***, the ***bitter herbs***

We gaze at, but do not lift, the shankbone and recite:

Pesach—What is the reason for the Pesach sacrifice that our forefathers ate during the time of the Temple? Because the Holy One, Blessed be He, passed over the houses of our foreforefathers in Egypt, as it is stated: "You shall say, 'It is a Pesach sacrifice to Hashem, for He passed over the houses of the children of Israel in Egypt when he struck the Egyptians, and He saved our houses. And the people kneeled and prostrated themselves.'"

as stuck in your old ways as before. But don't despair. With every step you move closer to the edge."

So too, must we not get discouraged, but continuously do teshuva and work on self-improvement.

♦ ♦ ♦ ♦ ♦ ♦

עַל אַחַת כַּמָּה וְכַמָּה טוֹבָה כְפוּלָה וּמְכֻפֶּלֶת לַמָּקוֹם עָלֵינוּ

We express our appreciation to Hashem for the tremendous good that He did for us. Why, then, do we say "למקום עלינו—*to* the Almighty for us?" Shouldn't the Haggadah speak of the good *from* the Almighty—ממקום?

It is because Hashem enjoys the good He does for us. When Hashem gives Klal Yisroel good, it is good for Him as well. Much as a father delights in treating a child as much as the child enjoys the treat, Hashem Himself feels the satisfaction of the good He does for us.

This tremendous satisfaction stretches so far that it is as if the Almighty is doing the good to himself—He is doing it למקום—to the Almighty. Hashem Himself is the beneficiary!

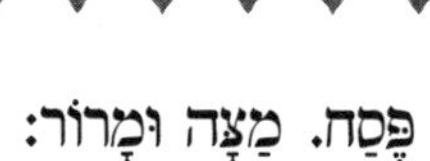

♦ ♦ ♦ ♦ ♦ ♦

פֶּסַח. מַצָּה וּמָרוֹר:

Rabbi Yisroel of Vizhnitz comments that the numerical sum (gematriya) of the words פסח מצה ומרור is 729, the same sum as the words קרע שטן—

The Seder leader lifts up the middle matzah and recites:

מַצָּה זוֹ שֶׁאָנוּ אוֹכְלִים, עַל שׁוּם מָה? עַל שׁוּם שֶׁלֹּא הִסְפִּיק בְּצֵקָם שֶׁל אֲבוֹתֵינוּ לְהַחֲמִיץ, עַד שֶׁנִּגְלָה עֲלֵיהֶם מֶלֶךְ מַלְכֵי הַמְּלָכִים, הַקָּדוֹשׁ בָּרוּךְ הוּא, וּגְאָלָם, שֶׁנֶּאֱמַר: וַיֹּאפוּ אֶת הַבָּצֵק, אֲשֶׁר הוֹצִיאוּ מִמִּצְרַיִם, עֻגֹת מַצּוֹת, כִּי לֹא חָמֵץ: כִּי גֹרְשׁוּ מִמִּצְרַיִם, וְלֹא יָכְלוּ לְהִתְמַהְמֵהַּ, וְגַם צֵדָה לֹא עָשׂוּ לָהֶם.

The Seder leader lifts up the marror and recites:

מָרוֹר זֶה שֶׁאָנוּ אוֹכְלִים, עַל שׁוּם מָה? עַל שׁוּם שֶׁמֵּרְרוּ הַמִּצְרִים אֶת חַיֵּי אֲבוֹתֵינוּ בְּמִצְרַיִם, שֶׁנֶּאֱמַר: וַיְמָרְרוּ אֶת חַיֵּיהֶם בַּעֲבֹדָה קָשָׁה, בְּחֹמֶר וּבִלְבֵנִים, וּבְכָל עֲבֹדָה בַּשָּׂדֶה: אֵת כָּל עֲבֹדָתָם, אֲשֶׁר עָבְדוּ בָהֶם בְּפָרֶךְ.

destroy the Satan.

On Rosh Hashanah, the Satan is destroyed by blowing the shofar. On Pesach, we can accomplish the same thing through the mitzvos of פסח מצה ומרור.

♦ ♦ ♦ ♦ ♦ ♦

Rabbi Yehoshua of Belz questions the order of Pesach's three signs. Shouldn't marror precede the others? After all, the bitterness of exile came long before the korban Pesach and the matzah!

Rabbi Yehoshua explains that the order of the signs teaches us that during galus we are blinded by our mortal comprehension of events. Our situation, and the situation of the entire world, seems extremely bitter. But after the redemption, we will suddenly be able to perceive that what we thought was so bitter was actually quite sweet, and was for our own benefit. It is only our human and limited perception that hides the good in the guise of pain and suffering.

The seder leader lifts up the middle matzah and recites:

Matzah—What is the reason we eat matzah? Because before our forefathers' dough had time to become leavened, the King of Kings, the Holy One, blessed is He, revealed Himself to them and redeemed them, as it is stated: "They baked the dough that they had taken out of Egypt as unleavened cakes, for it had not leavened, for they were driven out of Egypt and they could not tarry, and also they had not made provisions for themselves."

The seder leader lifts up the marror and recites:

Marror—What is the reason we eat bitter herbs? Because the Egyptians embittered our foreforefathers' lives in Egypt, as it is stated: "And they embittered their lives with hard labor, with clay and with bricks and with all kinds of labor in the fields, all their work that they worked with them with back-breaking labor."

The marror at the end of the list of signs shows us that the bitterness, too, was for our good, as were the korban Pesach and matzah.

Similarly, marror should precede matzah, for the Jews suffered first, before they baked matzah when they were redeemed. Why do we list marror last?

The truth is that, while the Jews were enslaved, they weren't aware of how severe their situation was. Only after they tasted matzah did they realized how bitter their lives were in galus. That is why the marror is eaten after the freedom of matzah is tasted.

We, too, seem to be comfortable in galus. We enjoy our civil liberties and our almost unprecedented communal prosperity. True, we have suffered jolts to our equanimity, but still, things seem to be going generally well. Galus sometimes seems to be tolerable, if not quite alright.

It is only after the Moshiach's arrival that we will see how bitter this galus was, and how much we missed.

♦ ♦ ♦ ♦ ♦ ♦

Rabbi Shmuel of Slonim, in *Divrei Shmuel*, teaches the same lesson from

בְּכָל דּוֹר וָדוֹר חַיָּב אָדָם לִרְאוֹת אֶת עַצְמוֹ, כְּאִלּוּ הוּא יָצָא מִמִּצְרָיִם, שֶׁנֶּאֱמַר: וְהִגַּדְתָּ לְבִנְךָ בַּיּוֹם הַהוּא לֵאמֹר: בַּעֲבוּר זֶה עָשָׂה יְיָ לִי, בְּצֵאתִי מִמִּצְרָיִם. לֹא אֶת אֲבוֹתֵינוּ בִּלְבָד, גָּאַל הַקָּדוֹשׁ בָּרוּךְ הוּא, אֶלָּא אַף אוֹתָנוּ גָּאַל עִמָּהֶם, שֶׁנֶּאֱמַר: וְאוֹתָנוּ הוֹצִיא מִשָּׁם, לְמַעַן הָבִיא אֹתָנוּ, לָתֶת לָנוּ אֶת הָאָרֶץ אֲשֶׁר נִשְׁבַּע לַאֲבֹתֵינוּ.

We lift our cup of wine, cover the matzos, and recite:

לְפִיכָךְ אֲנַחְנוּ חַיָּבִים לְהוֹדוֹת, לְהַלֵּל, לְשַׁבֵּחַ, לְפָאֵר, לְרוֹמֵם, לְהַדֵּר, לְבָרֵךְ, לְעַלֵּה וּלְקַלֵּס, לְמִי שֶׁעָשָׂה לַאֲבוֹתֵינוּ וְלָנוּ אֶת כָּל הַנִּסִּים הָאֵלּוּ. הוֹצִיאָנוּ מֵעַבְדוּת לְחֵרוּת, מִיָּגוֹן לְשִׂמְחָה, וּמֵאֵבֶל לְיוֹם טוֹב, וּמֵאֲפֵלָה לְאוֹר גָּדוֹל, וּמִשִּׁעְבּוּד לִגְאֻלָּה. וְנֹאמַר לְפָנָיו שִׁירָה חֲדָשָׁה. הַלְלוּיָהּ:

פ י ר ו ש

a verse in Shir Hamaalos. The posuk says—"בשוב ה׳ את שיבת ציון היינו כחולמים—When Hashem will return the captivity of Zion, we will be like dreamers." Why dreamers?

We may find ourselves in a terrible situation and experience horrific pain and suffering, only to suddenly awaken and realize that our experience was only an illusion.

Returning to Zion, too, will be an awakening. We'll suddenly realize that all we have lived through and suffered was simply a dream.

♦ ♦ ♦ ♦ ♦ ♦

בְּכָל דּוֹר וָדוֹר חַיָּב אָדָם לִרְאוֹת אֶת עַצְמוֹ

Rabbi Shlomo HaCohen Rabinowitz of Radomsk in his sefer, *Tiferes Shlomo,* says that we must always keep in mind our task in this world of

In every generation, it is one's duty to regard oneself as if he himself had come out of Egypt, as it is stated: "And you shall tell your son on that day, saying, 'Because of this, Hashem did this for me when I went out of Egypt.'" Not only our foreforefathers did the Holy One, blessed is He, redeem, but He redeemed us, too, along with them, as it is stated: "And He brought us out of there so that He might bring us, to give us the land that He promised to our foreforefathers."

We lift our cup of wine, cover the matzos, and recite:

Therefore it is our duty to thank, praise, laud, glorify, exalt, honor, bless, extol, and adore Him Who performed all these miracles for our foreforefathers and for us. He brought us out from slavery to freedom, from anguish to joy, from mourning to celebration, from darkness to great light, from bondage to redemption. Let us therefore, sing before Him a new song. Hallelujah!

♦ פירוש ♦

constantly evaluating our deeds to determine if we are reaching our potential and behaving as we should. This is not an easy task, for it is difficult to accurately assess one's faults.

Therefore, he advises us to enlist a spiritual person's assistance. This person will admonish us whenever necessary, and keep us on the proper path. It is, however, our job to accept the counsel we have sought.

♦ ♦ ♦ ♦ ♦ ♦

The Satmar Rebbe zt"l established a system where chassidim would admonish each other whenever they saw something amiss. A crucial part of the program was the provision that the one being admonished neither defend nor answer his or her reprover in any way, as a response would lessen the rebuke's effect.

♦ ♦ ♦ ♦ ♦ ♦

הַלְלוּיָהּ. הַלְלוּ עַבְדֵי יְיָ. הַלְלוּ אֶת שֵׁם יְיָ. יְהִי שֵׁם יְיָ מְבֹרָךְ מֵעַתָּה וְעַד עוֹלָם: מִמִּזְרַח שֶׁמֶשׁ עַד מְבוֹאוֹ. מְהֻלָּל שֵׁם יְיָ. רָם עַל כָּל גּוֹיִם יְיָ. עַל הַשָּׁמַיִם כְּבוֹדוֹ: מִי כַּיְיָ אֱלֹהֵינוּ. הַמַּגְבִּיהִי לָשָׁבֶת: הַמַּשְׁפִּילִי לִרְאוֹת בַּשָּׁמַיִם וּבָאָרֶץ: מְקִימִי מֵעָפָר דָּל. מֵאַשְׁפֹּת יָרִים אֶבְיוֹן: לְהוֹשִׁיבִי עִם נְדִיבִים. עִם נְדִיבֵי עַמּוֹ: מוֹשִׁיבִי עֲקֶרֶת הַבַּיִת אֵם הַבָּנִים שְׂמֵחָה. הַלְלוּיָהּ:

♦ פ י ר ו ש ♦

לְפִיכָךְ אֲנַחְנוּ חַיָּבִים לְהוֹדוֹת, לְהַלֵּל

Why don't we make a blessing on the mitzvah of recounting *yetzias* Mitzrayim, as we do on other mitzvos?

Rabbi Asher ben Yechiel, in his 13th century compilation of responsa, *Teshuvos HaRosh*, says that because סיפור יציאת מצרים is a mitzvah without bounds we say no blessing. One can expound on the miracles endlessly.

This is also why we don't make a blessing on the mitzvah of thanking Hashem. We could never fulfill our obligations and stop thanking our Creator!

♦ ♦ ♦ ♦ ♦ ♦

מִיגּוֹן לְשִׂמְחָה

HaGaon HaRav Elchonon Wasserman zt"l asks: How can one make the transition from sadness to joy?

At a joyous dedication of the Baranovich Yeshiva, R' Elchonon addressed the crowd with harsh words of mussar. He then explained why he chose to rebuke even when it would subdue the joy of the occasion.

He told about a prince who fell into a deep depression. The king tried everything to make his son happy. Still, the young man remained melancholy. In an effort to rid the prince of his gloom, the king arranged a gala celebration. He ordered the finest wines, the most elegant foods, and the liveliest music. He then invited thousands of guests in the hope that the party would lift his son's spirits.

Hallelujah! Praise, you servants of Hashem, praise the name of Hashem. May the name of Hashem be blessed from now and unto eternity. From the rising of the sun until its setting, the name of Hashem is praised. Hashem is high above all nations; His glory is above the heavens. Who is like Hashem, our God, Who dwells on high? Who lowers His eyes to look upon the heavens and the earth? He lifts the pauper from the dust, from the dung heap He raises the needy; to seat him with princes, with the princes of His people. He seats the barren woman of the house as a happy mother of children. Hallelujah!

♦ פ י ר ו ש ♦

But while the guests reveled, sang and danced, the prince sat alone, miserable as ever.

"What should we do? How can we help him?" cried the king to his advisors.

The wise men of the kingdom presented their suggestions. One said to call a juggler. The other suggested a jester. The King listened to his advisors, but no matter who the king called, the prince could not be drawn out of his gloom. Finally, one advisor made a suggestion. "Have the band play a sad, soulful song," he said.

The others protested. "He's sad enough!" they countered. Still, the king decided there was nothing to lose. The band began to play a slow, haunting tune. Suddenly, the prince looked up, tears rolling down his cheeks. All of the gloom he had been feeling poured forth, as he sighed and wept to the music.

The wise men of the kingdom shook their heads at the one who had made the suggestion. He had only made the situation worse!

Just then, the advisor signaled to the musicians to step up the music. A cheerful tune suddenly danced through the air. And then, to everyone's surprise, a smile broke on the prince's face. He tapped his foot to the music, and soon he was clapping his hands, and joined the joyful circle of dancers.

R' Elchonon explained that when people are despondent, they will not respond to the joy around them. One who is in a state of simcha must approach those enmeshed in gloom and draw them from their level of misery to true joy.

בְּצֵאת יִשְׂרָאֵל מִמִּצְרָיִם, בֵּית יַעֲקֹב מֵעַם לֹעֵז: הָיְתָה יְהוּדָה לְקָדְשׁוֹ. יִשְׂרָאֵל מַמְשְׁלוֹתָיו: הַיָּם רָאָה וַיָּנֹס, הַיַּרְדֵּן יִסֹּב לְאָחוֹר: הֶהָרִים רָקְדוּ כְאֵילִים. גְּבָעוֹת כִּבְנֵי צֹאן: מַה לְּךָ הַיָּם כִּי תָנוּס. הַיַּרְדֵּן תִּסֹּב לְאָחוֹר: הֶהָרִים תִּרְקְדוּ כְאֵילִים. גְּבָעוֹת כִּבְנֵי צֹאן: מִלִּפְנֵי אָדוֹן חוּלִי אָרֶץ. מִלִּפְנֵי אֱלוֹהַּ יַעֲקֹב: הַהֹפְכִי הַצּוּר אֲגַם מָיִם. חַלָּמִישׁ לְמַעְיְנוֹ מָיִם.

◆ פירוש ◆

In the story, the slow music mirrored the prince's feelings and thus allowed him to express himself. Once he was enabled to give expression to his sad feelings, he was then able to enjoy the happiness of the moment with the upbeat music. So too, R' Elchonon wanted the people to be able to fully appreciate the happiness of the moment. He therefore first spoke words of mussar, which inspired the people to elevate themselves, so that they could truly celebrate.

R' Elchonon believed that, at a time of happiness, mussar can bring people to another level, because when we are joyous our hearts are open and we are accessible.

The Malbim once asked: why do people cry when they are happy? He responded that we cry because we know that the moment of happiness won't last. So at times of happiness there is always an intermingling of emotions.

◆ ◆ ◆ ◆ ◆ ◆

הַמַּשְׁפִּילִי לִרְאוֹת

The Kozhnitzer Maggid says this verse refers to the humble. המשפילי—One who lowers oneself and is humble; לראות—will merit to see Hashem's greatness.

Matzah, the bread that has not risen, teaches us the same lesson of humility. What is forbidden is chametz; inflated, leavened, and high. By learning the lesson of the flat, modest matzah, we too will merit to see Hashem's greatness.

◆ ◆ ◆ ◆ ◆ ◆

When Israel left Egypt, the house of Jacob left a people of a strange tongue, Judah became His holy nation, Israel His dominion. The sea saw and fled; the Jordan turned backwards. The mountains danced like rams, hills like young sheep. What frightens you, O sea, that you flee? O Jordan, that you turn backwards? You mountains, that you dance like rams; you hills, like young sheep? From before the Master, Who created the earth, from before the God of Jacob, Who transforms the rock into a pond of water, the flint into a fountain of water.

◆ פירוש ◆

Once, at a large communal gathering, the host began to introduce the Tzimper Rav, HaGaon HaRav Moshe Dovid Ostreicher, who came from a small town, Tzimp, bordering Munkacz, in Hungary, and lived on the Lower East side of Manhattan (circa early 1900's), who was to be the next speaker. The host began to praise the Tzimper Rav, using accolades which made the exceedingly humble Rav completely uncomfortable. With each word, the Tzimper Rav began sinking lower and lower into his chair. By the time the man concluded, they found the Tzimper Rav actually sitting under the dais.

◆ ◆ ◆ ◆ ◆ ◆

הַיָּם רָאָה וַיָּנֹס

What did the water see that made it flee? Chazal tell us that the water saw Yosef's casket.

Rabbi Avraham Borenstein, in his book *Shem M'Shmuel* explains: Although Yosef HaTzaddik was Egypt's leader, he maintained his piety, remaining the same person he was when he was growing up in Yaakov Avinu's home. He did not only lead Egypt; he led the Jewish People by modeling how to face life's trials. It was the merit of Yosef's adhering to the proper path in challenging times that caused the sea to split.

We all should be aware of our own internal powers to stand firm in the face of the multitude of lures and traps set before us.

In *Michtav M'Eliyahu* we are told that when we pray each morning: "and do not bring us to a nisayon (a test); and [do] not [bring us] to

The cup is lifted and the matzos are covered during the recitation of the following blessing:

בָּרוּךְ אַתָּה יְיָ, אֱלֹהֵינוּ מֶלֶךְ הָעוֹלָם, אֲשֶׁר גְּאָלָנוּ וְגָאַל אֶת אֲבוֹתֵינוּ מִמִּצְרַיִם, וְהִגִּיעָנוּ לַלַּיְלָה הַזֶּה, לֶאֱכָל בּוֹ מַצָּה וּמָרוֹר. כֵּן, יְיָ אֱלֹהֵינוּ וֵאלֹהֵי אֲבוֹתֵינוּ, יַגִּיעֵנוּ לְמוֹעֲדִים וְלִרְגָלִים אֲחֵרִים, הַבָּאִים לִקְרָאתֵנוּ לְשָׁלוֹם. שְׂמֵחִים בְּבִנְיַן עִירֶךָ, וְשָׂשִׂים בַּעֲבוֹדָתֶךָ, וְנֹאכַל שָׁם מִן הַזְּבָחִים וּמִן הַפְּסָחִים (במוצאי שבת אומרים מִן הַפְּסָחִים וּמִן הַזְּבָחִים), אֲשֶׁר יַגִּיעַ דָּמָם, עַל קִיר מִזְבַּחֲךָ לְרָצוֹן, וְנוֹדֶה לְךָ שִׁיר חָדָשׁ עַל גְּאֻלָּתֵנוּ, וְעַל פְּדוּת נַפְשֵׁנוּ: בָּרוּךְ אַתָּה יְיָ, גָּאַל יִשְׂרָאֵל:

בָּרוּךְ אַתָּה יְיָ, אֱלֹהֵינוּ מֶלֶךְ הָעוֹלָם, בּוֹרֵא פְּרִי הַגָּפֶן:

While reclining on our left side, we now drink the second cup of wine.

◆ פ י ר ו ש ◆

shame," our intention is to ask that we not receive a test that we would not be able to withstand.

◆ ◆ ◆ ◆ ◆ ◆

Throughout the ages we have longed for Moshiach, and at various times Moshiach has been momentarily revealed, in order to renew our hope that he will one day indeed arrive. Years ago, in Poland, the Chozeh of Lublin was asked by a devoted follower for a hint as to when Moshiach would come. The tzaddik told his follower to go to the railroad station at the end of town. He told him that early the next morning, before sunrise, a train would pull in and the first person to get off the train would be Moshiach. The chossid was so filled with anticipation he could not sleep that night. Instead, he waited at the train station throughout the night until the predawn train arrived. As the train finally pulled in, the chossid's heart raced. He could hardly wait to meet Moshiach. However, the first person to leave the train was a man who looked like a Polish nobleman in all of his finery. The chossid could

The cup is lifted and the matzos are covered during the recitation of the following blessing:

Blessed are You, Hashem our God, King of the universe, Who redeemed us and redeemed our forefathers from Egypt, and enabled us to reach this night that we may eat matzah and bitter herbs. Likewise, Hashem, our God and the God of our forefathers, enable us to celebrate festivals and holidays in peace, joyous in the building of Your city and happy in Your service. There we will partake of the sacrifices and from the Pesach sacrifices (*on motzei Shabbos substitute:* of the Pesach sacrifices and from the sacrifices) whose blood will be sprinkled upon the side of Your altar for Your acceptance. There we will sing a new song to You for our redemption and for the deliverance of our souls. Blessed are You, Hashem, Who redeemed Israel.

Blessed are You, Hashem our God, King of the universe, Who created the fruit of the vine.

While reclining on our left side, we now drink the second cup of wine.

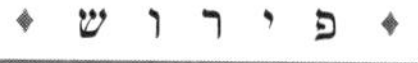

not believe that this was Moshiach. As the chossid stared at this person intently, he realized that it would be rude not to greet him. He therefore greeted the man with the words "Zhin dobri" ("good day" in Polish). The man responded with a curt reply and disappeared into the crowd.

Disappointed, the chossid immediately returned home to his Rebbe. As soon as the Rebbe saw the chossid's crestfallen face, he asked, "Didn't you meet Moshiach?" In a voice filled with sadness, the chossid responded, "No, the first person to get off the train was a Polish nobleman!" The Rebbe then asked, "So how did you greet him?" The chossid shrugged, "I said to him in Polish, 'Good morning.'" The Rebbe smiled and explained that that man really was Moshiach. If he had only had faith in the Rebbe's words and greeted him with a "shalom aleichem," it could have been an historic moment in time.

We too have a chance to meet Moshiach, but we have to greet him properly, by yearning daily for his arrival and greeting him with joy and song when he arrives.

רָחְצָה

We wash our hands and recite the customary blessing:

בָּרוּךְ אַתָּה יְיָ אֱלֹהֵינוּ מֶלֶךְ הָעוֹלָם, אֲשֶׁר קִדְּשָׁנוּ בְּמִצְוֹתָיו, וְצִוָּנוּ עַל נְטִילַת יָדָיִם:

מוֹצִיא. מַצָּה

The Seder leader takes the two whole matzos and the broken middle matzah, lifts them and recites:

בָּרוּךְ אַתָּה יְיָ, אֱלֹהֵינוּ מֶלֶךְ הָעוֹלָם, הַמּוֹצִיא לֶחֶם מִן הָאָרֶץ:

The Seder leader lets the lowest matzah slip from his hands and recites the following blessing (keeping in mind the matzah of the sandwich and the Afikomen when reciting the blessing):

בָּרוּךְ אַתָּה יְיָ, אֱלֹהֵינוּ מֶלֶךְ הָעוֹלָם, אֲשֶׁר קִדְּשָׁנוּ בְּמִצְוֹתָיו וְצִוָּנוּ עַל אֲכִילַת מַצָּה:

The Seder leader then distributes at least an olive-sized portion (preferably two olive-sized portions) of the matzah to each of the assembled, and while reclining on our left side we eat the matzah.

♦ פ י ר ו ש ♦

מוֹצִיא. מַצָּה

HaGaon HaRav Elazar Menachem Mann Shach zt"l said: What is the difference between chametz and matzah? A moment of *hesech hadaas*. One moment of inadequate attention, and the matzah can turn into chametz!

The very first murder took place when Kayin and Hevel argued. R'

Rochtzah

We wash our hands and recite the customary blessing:

Blessed are You, Hashem our God, King of the universe, Who has sanctified us with His commandments, and commanded us concerning the washing of hands.

Motzi. Matzah

The Seder leader takes the two whole matzos and the broken middle matzah, lifts them and recites:

Blessed are You, Hashem our God, King of the universe, Who brought forth bread from the earth.

The Seder leader lets the lowest matzah slip from his hands and recites the following blessing (keeping in mind the matzah of the sandwich and the Afikomen when reciting the blessing):

Blessed are You, Hashem our God, King of the universe, Who has sanctified us with His commandments, and commanded us concerning the eating of matzah.

The Seder leader then distributes at least an olive-sized portion (preferably two olive-sized portions) of the matzah to each of the assembled, and while reclining on our left side we eat the matzah.

♦ פירוש ♦

Yehoshua says that they were arguing over where the Beis Hamikdash should be built. Kayin wanted it to be in his portion, and Hevel wanted it in his portion. The result? Murder.

If we consider the circumstances, we see that both Kayin and Hevel were spiritual people. They were both neviim, and shared a thirst for the Shechinah. How did their argument bring them to such a terrible sin? One moment of *hesech hadaas*. One moment of thoughtlessness,

מָרוֹר

We dip bitter herbs in charoses and recite the following blessing. The marror should be eaten without reclining, since it represents the bitterness of slavery.

בָּרוּךְ אַתָּה יְיָ אֱלֹהֵינוּ מֶלֶךְ הָעוֹלָם, אֲשֶׁר קִדְּשָׁנוּ בְּמִצְוֹתָיו וְצִוָּנוּ עַל אֲכִילַת מָרוֹר:

כּוֹרֵךְ

We dip the marror in charoses, place it between two pieces of matzos and as we hold it we make the following declaration:

זֵכֶר לְמִקְדָּשׁ כְּהִלֵּל: כֵּן עָשָׂה הִלֵּל בִּזְמַן שֶׁבֵּית הַמִּקְדָּשׁ הָיָה קַיָּם. הָיָה כּוֹרֵךְ פֶּסַח מַצָּה וּמָרוֹר וְאוֹכֵל בְּיַחַד. לְקַיֵּם מַה שֶּׁנֶּאֱמַר: עַל מַצּוֹת וּמְרוֹרִים יֹאכְלֻהוּ:

While reclining on our left side, we eat the matzah and marror sandwich.

◆ פירוש ◆

of allowing personal considerations to transcend reason, can yield catastrophic results.

◆ ◆ ◆ ◆ ◆ ◆

עַל אֲכִילַת מַצָּה

Eating matzah is a *segulah* for ridding us of our evil temptations. Reb Menachem Mendel of Rimanov interprets the words מוציא מצה to demonstrate this. מוציא מצה—The matzah removes temptation.

The Zohar says that there are two fundamental qualities in matzah. The first is that it is *michla d'mhaimenusah*—the "Food of Faith;" the

Maror

We dip bitter herbs in charoses and recite the following blessing. The marror should be eaten without reclining, since it represents the bitterness of slavery.

Blessed are You, Hashem our God, King of the universe, Who has sanctified us with His commandments, and commanded us concerning the eating of bitter herbs.

Korech

We dip the marror in charoses, place it between two pieces of matzos and as we hold it we make the following declaration:

In remembrance of the Temple, according to the custom of Hillel. This is what Hillel did at the time the Temple still stood. He would combine Pesach with matzah and marror and eat them together in order to fulfill that which is stated: "They shall eat it with matzah and marror."

While reclining on our left side, we eat the matzah and marror sandwich.

second is that it is *michla d'asvusa*—the "Food of Healing." On the first Seder night, the matzah is the "Food of Faith." On the second Seder night, the night the Seder is held only outside of Eretz Yisroel, the matzah becomes the "Food of Healing."

♦ ♦ ♦ ♦ ♦ ♦

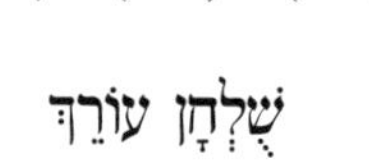

We do not always realize what tremendous kedusha we infuse into our tables with our *avodas* Hashem during our Shabbos and Yom Tov meals.

שֻׁלְחָן עוֹרֵךְ

We now eat the Seder meal, keeping in mind that the Afikomen must be eaten before midnight.

צָפוּן

Now we eat the portion of the broken matzah called the Afikomen that had been set aside at the beginning of the seder, during Yachatz.

בָּרֵךְ

The third cup of wine is now poured and grace after meals is recited.

שִׁיר הַמַּעֲלוֹת בְּשׁוּב יְיָ אֶת שִׁיבַת צִיּוֹן הָיִינוּ כְּחֹלְמִים: אָז יִמָּלֵא שְׂחוֹק פִּינוּ וּלְשׁוֹנֵנוּ רִנָּה אָז יֹאמְרוּ בַגּוֹיִם הִגְדִּיל יְיָ לַעֲשׂוֹת עִם אֵלֶּה: הִגְדִּיל יְיָ לַעֲשׂוֹת עִמָּנוּ הָיִינוּ שְׂמֵחִים: שׁוּבָה יְיָ אֶת שְׁבִיתֵנוּ כַּאֲפִיקִים בַּנֶּגֶב: הַזֹּרְעִים בְּדִמְעָה בְּרִנָּה יִקְצֹרוּ: הָלוֹךְ יֵלֵךְ וּבָכֹה נֹשֵׂא מֶשֶׁךְ הַזָּרַע בֹּא יָבֹא בְרִנָּה נֹשֵׂא אֲלֻמֹּתָיו:

♦ פ י ר ו ש ♦

Rabbi Mordechai Gifter zt"l was a world leader of Torah Jewry and the Rosh Yeshiva of the Telshe Yeshiva in Cleveland, Ohio for many years.

Once, when Rebbetzin Gifter wanted to replace their old, worn, wood dining room table, she asked the Rosh Yeshiva for his opinion on the matter.

Shulchan Orech

We now eat the Seder meal, keeping in mind that the Afikomen must be eaten before midnight.

Tzafun

Now we eat the portion of the broken matzah called the Afikomen that had been set aside at the beginning of the seder, during Yachatz.

Borech

The third cup of wine is now poured and grace after meals is recited.

A song of ascents. When Hashem brings back the returnees to Zion, we shall be like dreamers. Then our mouths will be filled with laughter and our tongues with songs of praise. Then they will say among the nations, "Hashem has done great things with these." Return us, O Hashem, from our captivity like streams in the desert. Those who sow with tears will reap with joyous song. He who goes along weeping, carrying valuable seeds, will return with joyous song carrying his sheaves.

♦ פירוש ♦

"For so many years, we sat at this table on Shabbos and Yom Tov," he said. "We said divrei Torah. The bochurim sang zemiros and niggunim, and spoke in learning here. Chas v'shalom that we should get rid of it! It would be better to refurbish it, and make it look like new."

♦ ♦ ♦ ♦ ♦ ♦

If three or more males are present, the following introductory phrases are added. When ten or more males are present, the words in brackets are inserted as well.

The leader begins:

רַבּוֹתַי נְבָרֵךְ!

The others reply:

יְהִי שֵׁם יְיָ מְבֹרָךְ מֵעַתָּה וְעַד עוֹלָם.

The leader proceeds:

יְהִי שֵׁם יְיָ מְבֹרָךְ מֵעַתָּה וְעַד עוֹלָם.

בִּרְשׁוּת מָרָנָן וְרַבָּנָן וְרַבּוֹתַי, נְבָרֵךְ [אֱלֹהֵינוּ] שֶׁאָכַלְנוּ מִשֶּׁלּוֹ.

The others reply:

בָּרוּךְ [אֱלֹהֵינוּ] שֶׁאָכַלְנוּ מִשֶּׁלּוֹ וּבְטוּבוֹ חָיִינוּ.

The leader repeats:

בָּרוּךְ [אֱלֹהֵינוּ] שֶׁאָכַלְנוּ מִשֶּׁלּוֹ וּבְטוּבוֹ חָיִינוּ.

[בָּרוּךְ הוּא וּבָרוּךְ שְׁמוֹ:]

בָּרוּךְ אַתָּה יְיָ, אֱלֹהֵינוּ מֶלֶךְ הָעוֹלָם, הַזָּן אֶת הָעוֹלָם כֻּלּוֹ בְּטוּבוֹ בְּחֵן בְּחֶסֶד וּבְרַחֲמִים הוּא נוֹתֵן לֶחֶם לְכָל בָּשָׂר כִּי לְעוֹלָם חַסְדּוֹ. וּבְטוּבוֹ הַגָּדוֹל תָּמִיד לֹא חָסַר לָנוּ, וְאַל יֶחְסַר לָנוּ מָזוֹן לְעוֹלָם וָעֶד. בַּעֲבוּר שְׁמוֹ הַגָּדוֹל, כִּי הוּא אֵל זָן וּמְפַרְנֵס לַכֹּל וּמֵטִיב לַכֹּל, וּמֵכִין מָזוֹן לְכָל בְּרִיּוֹתָיו אֲשֶׁר בָּרָא. בָּרוּךְ אַתָּה יְיָ, הַזָּן אֶת הַכֹּל:

◆ פ י ר ו ש ◆

בָּרֵךְ
הָיִינוּ כְּחֹלְמִים

The Skolya Rebbe, HaGaon HaRav R' Dovid Yitzchok Isaac M'Skolya zt"l, described the current world situation as one where other nations hate the Jews. When Moshiach comes, other nations will realize that if it were not for the Jews, the Torah we study and the mitzvos we perform, they would never have survived. It is the Jews who have safeguarded the world for everyone.

If three or more males are present, the following introductory phrases are added. When ten or more males are present, the words in brackets are inserted as well.

The leader begins:

Gentleman, let us say grace.

The others reply:

May the name of Hashem be blessed from now until eternity.

The leader proceeds:

With your permission, let us bless [our God] of Whose bounty we have partaken.

The others reply:

Blessed is [our God] of Whose bounty we have partaken and through whose goodness we live.

The leader repeats:

Blessed is [our God] of Whose bounty we have partaken and through Whose goodness we live.

[Blessed is He and Blessed is His Name.]

Blessed are You, Hashem, our God, King of the universe, Who sustains the entire world with His goodness, with grace, with kindness, and with mercy. He provides food for all flesh, for His kindness is eternal. And through His abundant goodness, we have never lacked, and we will never lack food forever and ever, for the sake of His great Name. For He is God Who nourishes and supports all, and does good for all, and prepares food for all His creatures whom He has created. Blessed are You, God, Who sustains all.

The word כחולמים hints at this fact. "כחולמים" can be divided into the words כחול מים meaning like the sand at the sea. Just like the sand protects the land from the sea—forming a barrier and keeping the water within its boundaries—so too the Jewish nation protects the entire world.

The verse continues. "אז יאמרו בגוים הגדיל ה' לעשות אם אלה—Then they will say in the nations, Hashem has done great things with these people." The other nations will recognize, admit, and acknowledge that the Jewish People have sustained the world.

נוֹדֶה לְּךָ יְיָ אֱלֹהֵינוּ עַל שֶׁהִנְחַלְתָּ לַאֲבוֹתֵינוּ, אֶרֶץ חֶמְדָּה טוֹבָה וּרְחָבָה, וְעַל שֶׁהוֹצֵאתָנוּ יְיָ אֱלֹהֵינוּ מֵאֶרֶץ מִצְרַיִם, וּפְדִיתָנוּ, מִבֵּית עֲבָדִים, וְעַל בְּרִיתְךָ שֶׁחָתַמְתָּ בִּבְשָׂרֵנוּ, וְעַל תּוֹרָתְךָ שֶׁלִּמַּדְתָּנוּ, וְעַל חֻקֶּיךָ שֶׁהוֹדַעְתָּנוּ וְעַל חַיִּים חֵן וָחֶסֶד שֶׁחוֹנַנְתָּנוּ, וְעַל אֲכִילַת מָזוֹן שָׁאַתָּה זָן וּמְפַרְנֵס אוֹתָנוּ תָּמִיד, בְּכָל יוֹם וּבְכָל עֵת וּבְכָל שָׁעָה:

וְעַל הַכֹּל יְיָ אֱלֹהֵינוּ אֲנַחְנוּ מוֹדִים לָךְ, וּמְבָרְכִים אוֹתָךְ, יִתְבָּרַךְ שִׁמְךָ בְּפִי כָּל חַי תָּמִיד לְעוֹלָם וָעֶד. כַּכָּתוּב, וְאָכַלְתָּ וְשָׂבָעְתָּ, וּבֵרַכְתָּ אֶת יְיָ אֱלֹהֶיךָ עַל הָאָרֶץ הַטֹּבָה אֲשֶׁר נָתַן לָךְ. בָּרוּךְ אַתָּה יְיָ, עַל הָאָרֶץ וְעַל הַמָּזוֹן:

רַחֵם נָא יְיָ אֱלֹהֵינוּ, עַל יִשְׂרָאֵל עַמֶּךָ, וְעַל יְרוּשָׁלַיִם עִירֶךָ, וְעַל צִיּוֹן מִשְׁכַּן כְּבוֹדֶךָ, וְעַל מַלְכוּת בֵּית דָּוִד מְשִׁיחֶךָ, וְעַל הַבַּיִת הַגָּדוֹל וְהַקָּדוֹשׁ שֶׁנִּקְרָא שִׁמְךָ עָלָיו. אֱלֹהֵינוּ, אָבִינוּ, רְעֵנוּ, זוּנֵנוּ, פַּרְנְסֵנוּ, וְכַלְכְּלֵנוּ, וְהַרְוִיחֵנוּ, וְהַרְוַח לָנוּ יְיָ אֱלֹהֵינוּ מְהֵרָה מִכָּל צָרוֹתֵינוּ, וְנָא, אַל תַּצְרִיכֵנוּ יְיָ אֱלֹהֵינוּ, לֹא לִידֵי מַתְּנַת בָּשָׂר וָדָם, וְלֹא לִידֵי הַלְוָאָתָם. כִּי אִם לְיָדְךָ הַמְּלֵאָה, הַפְּתוּחָה, הַקְּדוֹשָׁה וְהָרְחָבָה, שֶׁלֹּא נֵבוֹשׁ וְלֹא נִכָּלֵם לְעוֹלָם וָעֶד:

פירוש

רַחֵם נָא ה׳ אֱ-לֹהֵינוּ, עַל יִשְׂרָאֵל עַמֶּךָ, וְעַל יְרוּשָׁלַיִם עִירֶךָ

Both Yisroel and Yerushalayim are mentioned here. It is similar to the *nusach* said on *leil* Shabbos, which also includes both Yisroel and Yerushalayim—"הפורש סכת שלום עלינו ועל כל עמו ישראל—Who spreads the shelter of peace upon us, upon all of His people Israel and upon Yerushalayim."

We thank You, Hashem, our God, for bequeathing to our fathers a desirable, good, and spacious land; and for taking us, Hashem, our God, out of the land of Egypt, and redeeming us from the house of bondage, and for Your covenant that You sealed in our flesh, and for Your Torah that You taught us, and for Your statutes which You made known to us, and for the life, grace, and kindness which You bestowed upon us, and for the partaking of the food with which You feed and support us continually, every day, at all times, and at every hour.

For everything, Hashem, our God, we thank You and bless You. Blessed be Your Name in the mouth of all the living, continuously, forever and ever. As it is written, "And you will eat and be satisfied, and you shall bless Hashem, your God, for the good land that He has given you." Blessed are You, Hashem, for the land and for the food.

Have mercy, Hashem, our God, on Israel your people, and on Jerusalem your city, and on Zion the dwelling-place of Your glory, and on the dynasty of the house of David, Your anointed, and on the great and holy house upon which Your Name is called. Our God, our Father, tend us, feed us, support us and maintain us, and grant us relief. Relieve us, Hashem, our God, quickly from all our troubles. And please do not make us dependent, Hashem, our God, upon the gifts of flesh and blood nor upon their loans, but only upon Your full, open, holy, and ample hand, so that we should not be ashamed or disgraced, forever and ever.

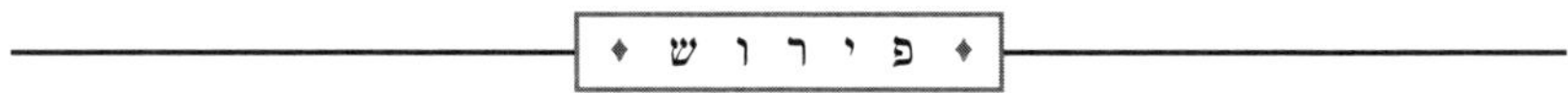

R' Yosef Chaim Sonnenfeld asks why we need to ask for peace for both Yisroel and Yerushalayim. He explains that Yerushalayim needs a particular *sholom*, a special שמירה עליונה—Heavenly protection.

Abba Issi said, in the name of Shmuel Hakatan (Derech Eretz Zuta 9): The world is like a human eye, and the white of the eye is the ocean sur-

On Shabbos add the following paragraph:

[**רְצֵה** וְהַחֲלִיצֵנוּ יְיָ אֱלֹהֵינוּ בְּמִצְוֹתֶיךָ וּבְמִצְוַת יוֹם הַשְּׁבִיעִי הַשַּׁבָּת הַגָּדוֹל וְהַקָּדוֹשׁ הַזֶּה. כִּי יוֹם זֶה גָּדוֹל וְקָדוֹשׁ הוּא לְפָנֶיךָ, לִשְׁבָּת בּוֹ וְלָנוּחַ בּוֹ בְּאַהֲבָה כְּמִצְוַת רְצוֹנֶךָ וּבִרְצוֹנְךָ הָנִיחַ לָנוּ יְיָ אֱלֹהֵינוּ, שֶׁלֹּא תְהֵא צָרָה וְיָגוֹן וַאֲנָחָה בְּיוֹם מְנוּחָתֵנוּ. וְהַרְאֵנוּ יְיָ אֱלֹהֵינוּ בְּנֶחָמַת צִיּוֹן עִירֶךָ, וּבְבִנְיַן יְרוּשָׁלַיִם עִיר קָדְשֶׁךָ, כִּי אַתָּה הוּא בַּעַל הַיְשׁוּעוֹת וּבַעַל הַנֶּחָמוֹת:]

אֱלֹהֵינוּ וֵאלֹהֵי אֲבוֹתֵינוּ, יַעֲלֶה וְיָבֹא וְיַגִּיעַ, וְיֵרָאֶה, וְיֵרָצֶה, וְיִשָּׁמַע, וְיִפָּקֵד, וְיִזָּכֵר זִכְרוֹנֵנוּ וּפִקְדוֹנֵנוּ, וְזִכְרוֹן אֲבוֹתֵינוּ, וְזִכְרוֹן מָשִׁיחַ בֶּן דָּוִד עַבְדֶּךָ, וְזִכְרוֹן יְרוּשָׁלַיִם עִיר קָדְשֶׁךָ, וְזִכְרוֹן כָּל עַמְּךָ בֵּית יִשְׂרָאֵל לְפָנֶיךָ, לִפְלֵיטָה לְטוֹבָה לְחֵן וּלְחֶסֶד וּלְרַחֲמִים, לְחַיִּים וּלְשָׁלוֹם בְּיוֹם חַג הַמַּצּוֹת הַזֶּה. זָכְרֵנוּ יְיָ אֱלֹהֵינוּ בּוֹ לְטוֹבָה. וּפָקְדֵנוּ בוֹ לִבְרָכָה. וְהוֹשִׁיעֵנוּ בוֹ לְחַיִּים, וּבִדְבַר יְשׁוּעָה וְרַחֲמִים, חוּס וְחָנֵּנוּ, וְרַחֵם עָלֵינוּ וְהוֹשִׁיעֵנוּ, כִּי אֵלֶיךָ עֵינֵינוּ, כִּי אֵל מֶלֶךְ חַנּוּן וְרַחוּם אָתָּה:

וּבְנֵה יְרוּשָׁלַיִם עִיר הַקֹּדֶשׁ בִּמְהֵרָה בְיָמֵינוּ. בָּרוּךְ אַתָּה יְיָ, בּוֹנֵה בְּרַחֲמָיו יְרוּשָׁלָיִם. אָמֵן

פ י ר ו ש

rounding the world. The iris is this continent, the pupil is Yerushalayim, and the image in the pupil is the Bais Hamikdash.

♦ ♦ ♦ ♦ ♦ ♦

On Shabbos add the following paragraph:

[Favor us and strengthen us, Hashem, our God, through Your commandments, and with the commandment of the seventh day, this great and holy Shabbos. For this day is great and holy before You, to refrain from work and to rest on this day, with love, following the command of Your desire. And may it be Your will, to grant us rest, Hashem, our God, so that there should be no trouble or sorrow or sighing on Your day of rest. Show us, Hashem, our God, the comfort of Zion, Your city, and the building of Jerusalem, the city of Your holiness, for You are the Master of salvation and the Master of consolations.]

Our God and the God of our fathers, may the remembrance and consideration of us, and the remembrance of our fathers, and the remembrance of the anointed son of David, Your servant, and the remembrance of Jerusalem, the city of Your holiness, and the remembrance of Your entire nation, the House of Israel, ascend, approach, reach, appear, be heard, be considered, and be remembered before you for deliverance, for good, for favor, for kindness, and for mercy, for life and for peace on this day of the holiday of matzos. Remember us on this day, Hashem, our God, for good, consider us upon it for blessing, and save us upon it for life.Through the promise of salvation and mercy, spare and favor us, have mercy on us and save us, for our eyes are turned to You, for You are a gracious and merciful God and King.

Rebuild Jerusalem, the holy city, speedily in our days. Blessed are You, Hashem, Who rebuilds Jerusalem in His mercy. Amen.

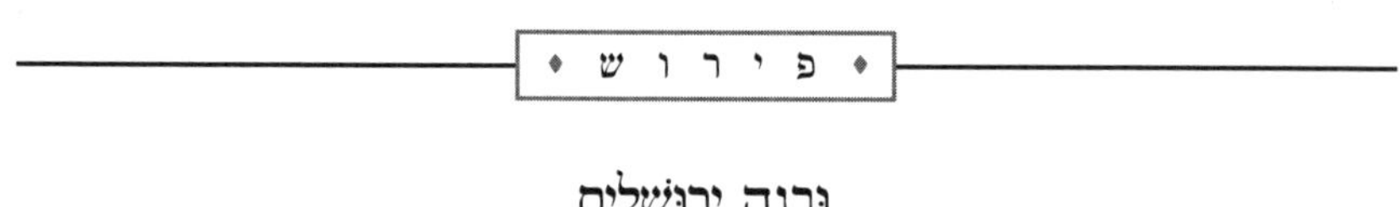

וּבְנֵה יְרוּשָׁלַיִם

Why do we include a prayer for Yerushalayim in our blessing after food?

When we eat, we realize that it is Hashem's chesed that enabled us to

בָּרוּךְ אַתָּה יְיָ אֱלֹהֵינוּ מֶלֶךְ הָעוֹלָם, הָאֵל אָבִינוּ, מַלְכֵּנוּ, אַדִּירֵנוּ בּוֹרְאֵנוּ, גּוֹאֲלֵנוּ, יוֹצְרֵנוּ, קְדוֹשֵׁנוּ קְדוֹשׁ יַעֲקֹב, רוֹעֵנוּ רוֹעֵה יִשְׂרָאֵל. הַמֶּלֶךְ הַטּוֹב, וְהַמֵּטִיב לַכֹּל, שֶׁבְּכָל יוֹם וָיוֹם הוּא הֵטִיב, הוּא מֵטִיב, הוּא יֵיטִיב לָנוּ. הוּא גְמָלָנוּ, הוּא גוֹמְלֵנוּ, הוּא יִגְמְלֵנוּ לָעַד לְחֵן וּלְחֶסֶד וּלְרַחֲמִים וּלְרֶוַח הַצָּלָה וְהַצְלָחָה בְּרָכָה וִישׁוּעָה, נֶחָמָה, פַּרְנָסָה וְכַלְכָּלָה, וְרַחֲמִים, וְחַיִּים וְשָׁלוֹם, וְכָל טוֹב, וּמִכָּל טוּב לְעוֹלָם אַל יְחַסְּרֵנוּ:

הָרַחֲמָן, הוּא יִמְלוֹךְ עָלֵינוּ לְעוֹלָם וָעֶד. הָרַחֲמָן, הוּא יִתְבָּרַךְ בַּשָּׁמַיִם וּבָאָרֶץ. הָרַחֲמָן, הוּא יִשְׁתַּבַּח לְדוֹר דּוֹרִים, וְיִתְפָּאַר בָּנוּ לָעַד וּלְנֵצַח נְצָחִים, וְיִתְהַדַּר בָּנוּ לָעַד וּלְעוֹלְמֵי עוֹלָמִים. הָרַחֲמָן, הוּא יְפַרְנְסֵנוּ בְּכָבוֹד. הָרַחֲמָן, הוּא יִשְׁבּוֹר עֻלֵּנוּ מֵעַל צַוָּארֵנוּ וְהוּא יוֹלִיכֵנוּ קוֹמְמִיּוּת לְאַרְצֵנוּ. הָרַחֲמָן, הוּא יִשְׁלַח לָנוּ בְּרָכָה מְרֻבָּה בַּבַּיִת הַזֶּה, וְעַל שֻׁלְחָן זֶה שֶׁאָכַלְנוּ עָלָיו. הָרַחֲמָן, הוּא יִשְׁלַח לָנוּ אֶת אֵלִיָּהוּ הַנָּבִיא זָכוּר לַטּוֹב, וִיבַשֶּׂר לָנוּ בְּשׂוֹרוֹת טוֹבוֹת יְשׁוּעוֹת וְנֶחָמוֹת.

◆ פירוש ◆

bring food onto our tables and that at this time the gates of Heaven are open. Therefore, it is an opportune time for us to ask Hashem, "Please open the gates a little wider, and give us the Beis Hamikdash."

◆ ◆ ◆ ◆ ◆ ◆

It is interesting to note that when we have the third and final future Bais Hamikdash all that has transpired throughout the generations will be revealed to us all. A fascinating gematriya is that the words בית המקדש equal 761, the same gematriya as לעיני כל ישראל—to the eyes of all Israel!

Blessed are You, Hashem, our God, King of the universe, the God of our fathers, our King, our Sovereign, our Creator, our Redeemer, our Maker, our Holy One, the Holy One of Jacob, our Shepherd, the Shepherd of Israel, the good King Who does good for all. Every single day He has done good, He does good, and He will do good for us. He has bestowed, He bestows, and He will bestow benefits upon us forever, with favor, kindness, mercy, and the relief of deliverance, success, blessing, salvation, comfort, sustenance and support, mercy, life, peace and all goodness.

May You never deprive us of anything good. May the Merciful One reign over us forever and ever! May the Merciful One be blessed in heaven and on earth! May the Merciful One be praised in every generation, and be glorified through us forever and ever, and be honored through us for all eternity. May the Merciful One support us in honor. May the Merciful One break our yoke off our necks and lead us upright into our land. May the Merciful One send a bountiful blessing in this household and upon this table upon which we have eaten. May the Merciful One send us Elijah the Prophet, remembered for good, and may he bring us good tidings, salvations, and consolations.

וְכָל טוּב, וּמִכָּל טוּב לְעוֹלָם אַל יְחַסְּרֵנוּ

Why is there a doubled expression of good?

HaGaon HaRav Shlomo Zalman Auerbach zt"l, explains: The first expression of good, וכל טוב, refers to Torah, the source of all good. There is no greater good in the world than Torah, and there can be nothing better for anyone than a true Torah life.

Still, we ask "ומכל טוב לעולם אל יחסרנו—what the world considers to be good, let us not lack." This refers to material goodness. We ask Hashem

at another's table (children at their parents' table add the words in parentheses):

הָרַחֲמָן, הוּא יְבָרֵךְ אֶת (אָבִי מוֹרִי) בַּעַל הַבַּיִת הַזֶּה, וְאֶת (אִמִּי מוֹרָתִי) בַּעֲלַת הַבַּיִת הַזֶּה,

at one's own table:

הָרַחֲמָן, הוּא יְבָרֵךְ אוֹתִי (וְאֶת אִשְׁתִּי\בַּעְלִי וְאֶת זַרְעִי וְאֶת כָּל אֲשֶׁר לִי)

all continue here:

אוֹתָם וְאֶת בֵּיתָם וְאֶת זַרְעָם וְאֶת כָּל אֲשֶׁר לָהֶם אוֹתָנוּ וְאֶת כָּל אֲשֶׁר לָנוּ, כְּמוֹ שֶׁנִּתְבָּרְכוּ אֲבוֹתֵינוּ, אַבְרָהָם יִצְחָק וְיַעֲקֹב: בַּכֹּל, מִכֹּל, כֹּל. כֵּן יְבָרֵךְ אוֹתָנוּ כֻּלָּנוּ יַחַד. בִּבְרָכָה שְׁלֵמָה, וְנֹאמַר אָמֵן:

◆ פ י ר ו ש ◆

that we not lack for anything, spiritual or material.

◆ ◆ ◆ ◆ ◆ ◆

בַּכֹּל, מִכֹּל, כֹּל

We can learn how to give tzedakah from these words. Who should collect for the poor? בכל means with all of the people. Thus everyone should collect money for the poor. Whom should you take from to give to the poor? מכל—from everyone. What should you give to the poor? כל—everything!

◆ ◆ ◆ ◆ ◆ ◆

The eminent tzaddik, R' Meir of Premishlan, was committed to the mitzvah of tzedakah. One of his rules was that he requested that no money which could be given to the poor remain in his house overnight.

One night he tossed and turned but could not fall asleep. The Rebbe

at another's table (children at their parents' table add the words in parentheses):

May the Merciful One bless (my father, my teacher,) the master of this house, and (my mother, my teacher,) the lady of this house.

at one's own table:

May the Merciful One bless me (and my wife/husband, my children and all that I have)

all continue here:

and all of those (participating in this meal), their households, their children, and all that they have, us and all that we have, just as our forefathers, Abraham, Isaac, and Jacob, were blessed in all things, from all things and with all things. So may He bless us all together with a complete blessing. Let us all say, Amen.

♦ פירוש ♦

knew that there must be some money, somewhere, which was his and had not been distributed among the poor. All the members of his household searched the entire house to see if there was money that had been inadvertently left over, but they couldn't find a thing.

He sent his gabbai to town to see if anyone had arrived that day to see the Rebbe. In one of the local inns, the gabbai found a visitor from a distant city. He had been on his way to see the Rebbe, but because of the lateness of the hour, he had changed his plans and decided to rest and visit the Rebbe on the next day. This man was carrying a *kvittel* and a *pidyon* (contribution) from a woman who wanted R' Meir to pray for her child. The man was told to come to the Rebbe and give him the *kvittel* and *pidyon* immediately. Since this money had been sent to R' Meir, it was as though it already was in his possession, and therefore the Rebbe could not sleep!

♦ ♦ ♦ ♦ ♦ ♦

In the sefer *Divrei Meir*, the words בכל מכל כל come from verses discussing Avraham, Yitzchok, and Yaakov. About Avraham it says, "וה' ברך את

בַּמָּרוֹם יְלַמְּדוּ עֲלֵיהֶם וְעָלֵינוּ זְכוּת, שֶׁתְּהֵא לְמִשְׁמֶרֶת שָׁלוֹם, וְנִשָּׂא בְרָכָה מֵאֵת יְיָ וּצְדָקָה מֵאֱלֹהֵי יִשְׁעֵנוּ, וְנִמְצָא חֵן וְשֵׂכֶל טוֹב בְּעֵינֵי אֱלֹהִים וְאָדָם:

On Shabbos add the following sentence:

[הָרַחֲמָן, הוּא יַנְחִילֵנוּ יוֹם שֶׁכֻּלּוֹ שַׁבָּת וּמְנוּחָה לְחַיֵּי הָעוֹלָמִים.]

הָרַחֲמָן, הוּא יַנְחִילֵנוּ יוֹם שֶׁכֻּלּוֹ טוֹב.

הָרַחֲמָן, הוּא יְזַכֵּנוּ לִימוֹת הַמָּשִׁיחַ וּלְחַיֵּי הָעוֹלָם הַבָּא.

מִגְדּוֹל יְשׁוּעוֹת מַלְכּוֹ, וְעֹשֶׂה חֶסֶד לִמְשִׁיחוֹ לְדָוִד וּלְזַרְעוֹ עַד עוֹלָם: עֹשֶׂה שָׁלוֹם בִּמְרוֹמָיו, הוּא יַעֲשֶׂה שָׁלוֹם, עָלֵינוּ וְעַל כָּל יִשְׂרָאֵל, וְאִמְרוּ אָמֵן:

יְראוּ אֶת יְיָ קְדֹשָׁיו, כִּי אֵין מַחְסוֹר לִירֵאָיו: כְּפִירִים רָשׁוּ וְרָעֵבוּ, וְדוֹרְשֵׁי יְיָ לֹא יַחְסְרוּ כָל טוֹב: הוֹדוּ לַייָ כִּי טוֹב, כִּי לְעוֹלָם חַסְדּוֹ: פּוֹתֵחַ אֶת יָדֶךָ, וּמַשְׂבִּיעַ לְכָל חַי רָצוֹן: בָּרוּךְ הַגֶּבֶר אֲשֶׁר יִבְטַח בַּייָ, וְהָיָה יְיָ מִבְטַחוֹ: נַעַר הָיִיתִי גַם זָקַנְתִּי וְלֹא רָאִיתִי צַדִּיק נֶעֱזָב, וְזַרְעוֹ מְבַקֶּשׁ לָחֶם: יְיָ עֹז לְעַמּוֹ יִתֵּן, יְיָ יְבָרֵךְ אֶת עַמּוֹ בַשָּׁלוֹם:

פ י ר ו ש

אברהם בכל—And Hashem blessed Avraham with everything" (Bereishis 24:3); about Yitzchok, "ואוכל מכל—I have eaten from everything" (Bereishis 27:33); and about Yaakov, "יש לי כל—I have everything" (Bereishis 33:11). The three verses in their proper order give us the words בכל מכל כל.

The Zohar says that throughout the centuries Yishmael has tried to

In heaven, may they plead our merits for a lasting peace, and may we receive a blessing from Hashem and justice from the God of our salvation, and may we find favor and good understanding in the eyes of God and man.

On Shabbos add the following sentence:

[May the Merciful One cause us to inherit the day that will be entirely one of Shabbos and rest for eternal life.]

May the Merciful One cause us to inherit a day of complete goodness.

May the Merciful One grant us the merit of living in the days of the Messiah and the life of the World-to-Come.

He is a tower of salvation to His king and shows kindness to His anointed, to David and to his descendants forever. He who makes peace in the heavens will make peace for us and all of Israel, say, Amen.

Fear Hashem—you—His holy ones, for nothing is lacking to those who fear Him. Young lions go poor and hungry, but those who seek Hashem will not be deprived of any good. Give thanks to Hashem for He is good—His kindness endures forever. You open Your hand and satisfy the desire of every living thing. Blessed is the man who trusts in Hashem and for whom Hashem is his support. I was young, and now I have grown old, and I have never seen a righteous man abandoned or his descendants begging for bread. Hashem will give strength to His nation; Hashem will bless His nation with peace.

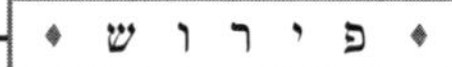

lay claim to rights as Avraham's heir. This is what has caused us to suffer so from his hands throughout our long galus and to this very day.

In defining Yishmael, the Torah tells us ידו בכל—his strength comes from בכל—Avraham Avinu. His end, however, will be יד כל בו—the hand of כל—Yaakov—will overcome and will save us from Yishmael. The Jewish people, with the power of Yaakov, will prevail over Yishmael.

While reclining on our left side, we recite the following blessing and drink the third cup of wine.

בָּרוּךְ אַתָּה יְיָ, אֱלֹהֵינוּ מֶלֶךְ הָעוֹלָם, בּוֹרֵא פְּרִי הַגָּפֶן:

We pour the fourth cup of wine and an extra cup for Eliyahu HaNavi (Elijah the Prophet). We open the door and recite the following:

שְׁפֹךְ חֲמָתְךָ אֶל הַגּוֹיִם, אֲשֶׁר לֹא יְדָעוּךָ וְעַל מַמְלָכוֹת אֲשֶׁר בְּשִׁמְךָ לֹא קָרָאוּ: כִּי אָכַל אֶת יַעֲקֹב. וְאֶת נָוֵהוּ הֵשַׁמּוּ: שְׁפָךְ עֲלֵיהֶם זַעְמֶךָ, וַחֲרוֹן אַפְּךָ יַשִּׂיגֵם: תִּרְדֹּף בְּאַף וְתַשְׁמִידֵם, מִתַּחַת שְׁמֵי יְיָ:

The door is now closed.

פירוש

ה׳ עֹז לְעַמּוֹ יִתֵּן

The 19th century tzaddik and chasidic leader, Rebbi Moshe Leib of Sassov asked, "What is the connection between the first part of the posuk, "ה׳ עוז לעמו יתן—Hashem should grant His nation strength," and the second part of the posuk, "ה׳ יברך את עמו בשלום—Hashem should bless His nation with peace"?

He explains that when people fall ill, chas v'shalom, they become quarrelsome and argumentative.

We ask Hashem that He grant His nation strength—that He make Klal Yisroel healthy and strong. Then, we will be blessed with perfect harmony.

◆ ◆ ◆ ◆ ◆ ◆

שְׁפֹךְ חֲמָתְךָ

It is customary to open the door during the recital of שפך חמתך to demonstrate that the Seder night is *Leil Shimurim*—"the guarded night." The Sfas Emes explains that the term *Leil Shimurim* is plural, to teach that the night was guarded not only in Egypt; it is guarded yearly,

While reclining on our left side, we recite the following blessing and drink the third cup of wine.

Blessed are you, Hashem, our God, King of the universe, Who created the fruit of the vine.

We pour the fourth cup of wine and an extra cup for Eliyahu HaNavi (Elijah the Prophet). We open the door and recite the following:

Pour out Your wrath upon the nations that do not know You and upon the kingdoms that did not call out in Your name. For they devoured Jacob and made his dwelling desolate. Pour Your fury upon them, and may Your burning wrath overtake them. Pursue them with fury and destroy them from under the heavens of Hashem.

The door is now closed.

♦ פ י ר ו ש ♦

throughout every generation.

♦ ♦ ♦ ♦ ♦ ♦

Eliyahu HaNavi visits Jews in two instances. He comes to the Pesach Seder and he comes to every bris milah. On both occasions, we prepare special items in his honor. At a bris milah, we honor him with the *kisei shel Eliyahu,* the seat reserved for Eliyahu HaNavi, and on Pesach, we honor him with the *kos shel Eliyahu*—Eliyahu HaNavi's cup. At the Seder, we do one thing more, we open the door for Eliyahu. Why the extra step?

At a bris milah, we know that Eliyah HaNavi will attend. It is unnecessary to open the door, because Eliyahu HaNavi will come and perform his task, regardless.

At the Seder, however, the *kos shel Eliyahu* is the Cup of Redemption. It is the fifth cup, the one that symbolizes our return to Eretz Yisroel. We know that the geulah cannot take place without a tremendous effort on our part. We must exhibit profound emunah in the coming of Moshiach before the geulah can take place.

That is why we open the door for Eliyahu HaNavi. We are displaying our emunah that this time, Eliyahu HaNavi will herald Moshiach's arrival. We hope that our emunah will bear fruit, and we will merit the geulah.

הַלֵּל

לֹא לָנוּ יְיָ לֹא לָנוּ כִּי לְשִׁמְךָ תֵּן כָּבוֹד, עַל חַסְדְּךָ עַל אֲמִתֶּךָ. לָמָּה יֹאמְרוּ הַגּוֹיִם, אַיֵּה נָא אֱלֹהֵיהֶם. וֵאלֹהֵינוּ בַשָּׁמָיִם כֹּל אֲשֶׁר חָפֵץ עָשָׂה. עֲצַבֵּיהֶם כֶּסֶף וְזָהָב, מַעֲשֵׂה יְדֵי אָדָם. פֶּה לָהֶם וְלֹא יְדַבֵּרוּ, עֵינַיִם לָהֶם וְלֹא יִרְאוּ. אָזְנַיִם לָהֶם וְלֹא יִשְׁמָעוּ, אַף לָהֶם וְלֹא יְרִיחוּן. יְדֵיהֶם וְלֹא יְמִישׁוּן, רַגְלֵיהֶם וְלֹא יְהַלֵּכוּ, לֹא יֶהְגּוּ בִּגְרוֹנָם. כְּמוֹהֶם יִהְיוּ עֹשֵׂיהֶם, כֹּל אֲשֶׁר בֹּטֵחַ בָּהֶם: יִשְׂרָאֵל בְּטַח בַּייָ, עֶזְרָם וּמָגִנָּם הוּא. בֵּית אַהֲרֹן בִּטְחוּ בַייָ, עֶזְרָם וּמָגִנָּם הוּא. יִרְאֵי יְיָ בִּטְחוּ בַייָ, עֶזְרָם וּמָגִנָּם הוּא:

יְיָ זְכָרָנוּ יְבָרֵךְ, יְבָרֵךְ אֶת בֵּית יִשְׂרָאֵל, יְבָרֵךְ אֶת בֵּית אַהֲרֹן. יְבָרֵךְ יִרְאֵי יְיָ, הַקְּטַנִּים עִם הַגְּדֹלִים. יֹסֵף יְיָ עֲלֵיכֶם, עֲלֵיכֶם וְעַל בְּנֵיכֶם. בְּרוּכִים אַתֶּם לַייָ, עֹשֵׂה שָׁמַיִם וָאָרֶץ. הַשָּׁמַיִם שָׁמַיִם לַייָ, וְהָאָרֶץ נָתַן לִבְנֵי אָדָם. לֹא הַמֵּתִים יְהַלְלוּ יָהּ, וְלֹא כָּל יֹרְדֵי דוּמָה. וַאֲנַחְנוּ נְבָרֵךְ יָהּ, מֵעַתָּה וְעַד עוֹלָם, הַלְלוּיָהּ:

◆ פירוש ◆

הַשָּׁמַיִם שָׁמַיִם לַה׳

Rabbi Menachem Mendel of Kotzk would say that people should not concern themselves with the spiritual level of the heavens. That is, after all, Hashem's concern. They should, however, worry about the earth. The spiritual level of the earth is in our hands. We must see to it that the earth reaches to the heavens, becoming the greatest we can make it.

Many of the things that we worry about are beyond our scope. These are esoteric concerns which are solely in the domain of the Ribono Shel

Hallel

Not for us, O Hashem, not for us, but for Your name give honor, for Your kindness and for Your truthfulness. Why should the nations say, "Where is your God now?" But our God is in heaven; whatever He wishes, He does. Their idols are silver and gold, the handiwork of man. They have a mouth but they do not speak; they have eyes but they do not see. They have ears but they do not hear; they have a nose but they do not smell. Their hands are there—but they do not feel; their feet are there—but they do not walk; they do not murmur with their throat. Like them shall be those who make them, all who trust in them. Israel, trust in Hashem; He is their help and their shield. House of Aaron, trust in Hashem; He is their help and their shield. Those who fear Hashem, trust in Hashem; He is their help and their shield.

Hashem, Who remembered us, will bless—He will bless the house of Israel; He will bless the house of Aaron. He will bless those who fear Hashem, the small together with the great. May Hashem add upon you, upon you and upon your children. Blessed are you to Hashem, the Maker of heaven and earth. The heavens are heavens of Hashem, but the earth He gave to the children of men. Neither will the dead praise God, nor all those who descend to the grave. But we shall bless God from now until everlasting! Hallelujah!

♦ פירוש ♦

Olam (Master of the Universe). Those are the Heavens. We should be concerned with spiritual matters which are in our hands, here on earth. We have the ability to elevate the mundane and the earthly heavenward.

The famous tzaddik R' Nachman of Breslov was asked why he liked to utilize the medium of dancing in the service of Hashem. He answered, "Because when one dances, one lifts one's feet ever so slightly from the ground and momentarily one is that much closer to Heaven!"

אָהַבְתִּי כִּי יִשְׁמַע יְיָ, אֶת קוֹלִי תַּחֲנוּנָי. כִּי הִטָּה אָזְנוֹ לִי וּבְיָמַי אֶקְרָא: אֲפָפוּנִי חֶבְלֵי מָוֶת, וּמְצָרֵי שְׁאוֹל מְצָאוּנִי צָרָה וְיָגוֹן אֶמְצָא. וּבְשֵׁם יְיָ אֶקְרָא, אָנָּה יְיָ מַלְּטָה נַפְשִׁי. חַנּוּן יְיָ וְצַדִּיק, וֵאלֹהֵינוּ מְרַחֵם. שֹׁמֵר פְּתָאִים יְיָ דַּלּוֹתִי וְלִי יְהוֹשִׁיעַ. שׁוּבִי נַפְשִׁי לִמְנוּחָיְכִי, כִּי יְיָ גָּמַל עָלָיְכִי. כִּי חִלַּצְתָּ נַפְשִׁי מִמָּוֶת אֶת עֵינִי מִן דִּמְעָה, אֶת רַגְלִי מִדֶּחִי. אֶתְהַלֵּךְ לִפְנֵי יְיָ, בְּאַרְצוֹת הַחַיִּים. הֶאֱמַנְתִּי כִּי אֲדַבֵּר, אֲנִי עָנִיתִי מְאֹד. אֲנִי אָמַרְתִּי בְחָפְזִי כָּל הָאָדָם כֹּזֵב.

מָה אָשִׁיב לַייָ, כָּל תַּגְמוּלוֹהִי עָלָי. כּוֹס יְשׁוּעוֹת אֶשָּׂא, וּבְשֵׁם יְיָ אֶקְרָא. נְדָרַי לַייָ אֲשַׁלֵּם, נֶגְדָה נָּא לְכָל עַמּוֹ. יָקָר בְּעֵינֵי יְיָ הַמָּוְתָה לַחֲסִידָיו. אָנָּה יְיָ כִּי אֲנִי עַבְדֶּךָ אֲנִי עַבְדְּךָ, בֶּן אֲמָתֶךָ פִּתַּחְתָּ לְמוֹסֵרָי. לְךָ אֶזְבַּח זֶבַח תּוֹדָה וּבְשֵׁם יְיָ אֶקְרָא. נְדָרַי לַייָ אֲשַׁלֵּם נֶגְדָה נָּא לְכָל עַמּוֹ. בְּחַצְרוֹת בֵּית יְיָ בְּתוֹכֵכִי יְרוּשָׁלָיִם הַלְלוּיָהּ.

הַלְלוּ אֶת יְיָ, כָּל גּוֹיִם, שַׁבְּחוּהוּ כָּל הָאֻמִּים. כִּי גָבַר עָלֵינוּ חַסְדּוֹ, וֶאֱמֶת יְיָ לְעוֹלָם הַלְלוּיָהּ:

◆ פירוש ◆

כִּי גָבַר עָלֵינוּ חַסְדּוֹ

Rabbi Aharon Perlow in his Torah commentary, *Bais Aharon*, comments that the word גבר comes from the word gevurah, meaning strength. Hashem's strength connotes *middas hadin*, which is the attribute of justice. Dovid HaMelech is saying כי גבר עלינו חסדו—even when Hashem metes out justice, חסדו—it is also chesed.

I wished that Hashem would hear my voice in my supplications. For He extended His ear to me, and I shall call out in my days. When bands of death surrounded me and the boundaries of the grave befell me, and I found trouble and grief, I called out in the name of Hashem, "Please, O Hashem, save my soul!" Hashem is gracious and righteous, and our God is merciful. Hashem protects the simple; when I was poor, He saved me. Return my soul to your rest, Hashem has dealt bountifully with you. You freed my soul from death, my eyes from tears, and my foot from stumbling. I shall walk before Hashem in the lands of the living. I kept my faith even when I said, "I am suffering deeply," and in my haste I said, "All men are liars."

How can I repay Hashem for all His favors toward me? I shall lift up a cup of salvations, and I shall call out in the name of Hashem. I shall pay my vows to Hashem in the presence of all His people. Precious in the eyes of Hashem is the death of His pious ones. Please, O Hashem, for I am Your servant—I am Your servant the son of Your maidservant—You have loosened my bonds. To You I shall slaughter a thanksgiving offering, and I shall call out in the name of Hashem. I shall pay my vows to Hashem now in the presence of all His people, in the courtyards of Hashem's house, in your midst, O Jerusalem. Hallelujah!

Praise Hashem, all nations. Laud Him, all peoples. His kindness has overwhelmed us, and the truth of Hashem is eternal. Hallelujah!

One Friday night, the 19th century chasidic master, Rabbi Boruch of Mezhibozh began to weep during zemiros. His grandson asked, —"Zeide, why are you crying?"

The tzaddik replied, "We just sang the words מודה אני לפניך ה׳ א-לוהי וא-לוהי אבותי על כל החסד אשר עשית עמדי ואשר אתה עתיד לעשות עמי which mean, I thank You, Hashem, for the chesed that You have done with me, and

הוֹדוּ לַיְיָ כִּי טוֹב,	כִּי לְעוֹלָם חַסְדּוֹ:
יֹאמַר נָא יִשְׂרָאֵל,	כִּי לְעוֹלָם חַסְדּוֹ:
יֹאמְרוּ נָא בֵית אַהֲרֹן,	כִּי לְעוֹלָם חַסְדּוֹ:
יֹאמְרוּ נָא יִרְאֵי יְיָ,	כִּי לְעוֹלָם חַסְדּוֹ:

מִן הַמֵּצַר קָרָאתִי יָּהּ, עָנָנִי בַמֶּרְחָב יָהּ. יְיָ לִי לֹא אִירָא, מַה יַּעֲשֶׂה לִי אָדָם. יְיָ לִי בְּעֹזְרָי, וַאֲנִי אֶרְאֶה בְשֹׂנְאָי. טוֹב לַחֲסוֹת בַּייָ, מִבְּטֹחַ בָּאָדָם. טוֹב לַחֲסוֹת בַּייָ מִבְּטֹחַ בִּנְדִיבִים. כָּל גּוֹיִם סְבָבוּנִי בְּשֵׁם יְיָ כִּי אֲמִילַם. סַבּוּנִי גַם סְבָבוּנִי בְּשֵׁם יְיָ כִּי אֲמִילַם. סַבּוּנִי כִדְבֹרִים דֹּעֲכוּ כְּאֵשׁ קוֹצִים, בְּשֵׁם יְיָ כִּי אֲמִילַם. דָּחֹה דְחִיתַנִי לִנְפֹּל, וַייָ עֲזָרָנִי. עָזִּי וְזִמְרָת יָהּ, וַיְהִי לִי לִישׁוּעָה. קוֹל רִנָּה וִישׁוּעָה בְּאָהֳלֵי צַדִּיקִים, יְמִין יְיָ עֹשָׂה חָיִל. יְמִין יְיָ רוֹמֵמָה, יְמִין יְיָ עֹשָׂה חָיִל. לֹא אָמוּת כִּי אֶחְיֶה, וַאֲסַפֵּר מַעֲשֵׂי יָהּ. יַסֹּר יִסְּרַנִּי יָּהּ, וְלַמָּוֶת לֹא נְתָנָנִי. פִּתְחוּ לִי שַׁעֲרֵי צֶדֶק ,אָבֹא בָם אוֹדֶה יָהּ. זֶה הַשַּׁעַר לַייָ, צַדִּיקִים יָבֹאוּ בוֹ.

פ י ר ו ש

for that which You will do for me.

"Why do we thank Hashem for the future? Because there may come a time when I will not recognize that a particular occurrence is a chesed. It may appear to me more like a difficulty, a test. That is why we thank Hashem in advance. We want to make sure that we have thanked Him for every chesed, whether or not we understand it. Everything Hashem does is a chesed, although we may not see it as such."

"But why are you crying?" asked the grandson. "If everything Hashem does is a chesed, we should rejoice!"

"Oy!" cried the tzaddik, "I cry I will be given chesed by my Father in

Give thanks to Hashem because He is good,
for His kindness is eternal.

Let Israel say, "For His kindness is eternal."
Let the house of Aaron say, "For His kindness is eternal."
Let those who fear Hashem say, "For His kindness is eternal."

In my distress I called God; God answered me with a vast expanse. Hashem is with me; I shall not fear. What can man do to me? Hashem is for me as my helper, and I shall gaze upon them that hate me. It is better to take refuge in Hashem than to trust in man. It is better to take refuge in Hashem than to trust in princes. All nations surround me; in the name of Hashem I shall cut them off. They encircle me, O they surround me; in the name of Hashem I shall cut them off. They encircle me like bees; they are extinguished like a thorn fire; in the name of Hashem I shall cut them off. You pushed me to fall, but Hashem helped me. Hashem is my strength and my song, and He has become my salvation. A voice of singing praises and salvation is in the tents of the righteous: "The right hand of Hashem deals valiantly. The right hand of Hashem is exalted; the right hand of Hashem deals valiantly." I shall not die but I shall live and tell the deeds of God. God has chastised me, but He has not delivered me to death. Open for me the gates of righteousness; I shall enter them and thank God. This is Hashem's gate; the righteous will enter therein.

♦ פירוש ♦

Heaven, and I may not notice the good in it. Woe to a son who doesn't appreciate his father's gift!"

♦ ♦ ♦ ♦ ♦ ♦

Rebbe Moshe Leib of Sassov understood the zemiros similarly, acknowledging that everything Hashem does is a chesed. But he added a request.

"The zemiros continue ועם כל בני ביתי—and with my entire household. Hashem, I know that everything You do is a chesed, whether or not we can understand it. Still, I beg You, let it be a chesed that my entire

The following four verses are each recited twice:

אוֹדְךָ כִּי עֲנִיתָנִי, וַתְּהִי לִי לִישׁוּעָה.
אֶבֶן מָאֲסוּ הַבּוֹנִים, הָיְתָה לְרֹאשׁ פִּנָּה.
מֵאֵת יְיָ הָיְתָה זֹּאת, הִיא נִפְלָאת בְּעֵינֵינוּ.
זֶה הַיּוֹם עָשָׂה יְיָ, נָגִילָה וְנִשְׂמְחָה בוֹ.

אָנָּא יְיָ הוֹשִׁיעָה נָּא: אָנָּא יְיָ הוֹשִׁיעָה נָּא:
אָנָּא יְיָ הַצְלִיחָה נָא: אָנָּא יְיָ הַצְלִיחָה נָא:

The following four verses are each recited twice:

בָּרוּךְ הַבָּא בְּשֵׁם יְיָ, בֵּרַכְנוּכֶם מִבֵּית יְיָ.
אֵל יְיָ וַיָּאֶר לָנוּ, אִסְרוּ חַג בַּעֲבֹתִים, עַד קַרְנוֹת הַמִּזְבֵּחַ.
אֵלִי אַתָּה וְאוֹדֶךָּ אֱלֹהַי אֲרוֹמְמֶךָּ.
הוֹדוּ לַייָ כִּי טוֹב, כִּי לְעוֹלָם חַסְדּוֹ.

פ י ר ו ש

household—even the unlearned and the little children, will be able to recognize. Let it be a chessed we can all understand."

We, too, beg Hashem "הראני ה' חסדך—Hashem, show us Your chesed. Let us all notice the good in everything; let it be a good that everyone can see clearly." Like we say on Rosh Hashanah, we ask Hashem to bless us with a *shanah tovah umesukah*—a good, sweet year. We know that it will be good, because everything from Hashem is good. But we ask Hashem to make it sweet, too.

♦ ♦ ♦ ♦ ♦ ♦

מִן הַמֵּצַר קָרָאתִי

A father's love for his child is so profound, he will not get upset if his

The following four verses are each recited twice:

I shall thank You because You have answered me, and You have become my salvation.
The stone that the builders rejected has become a cornerstone.
This is Hashem's doing; it is wondrous in our eyes.
This is the day that Hashem made; we shall exalt and rejoice.

Please, O Hashem, save us now!
Please, O Hashem, save us now!
Please, O Hashem, make us prosperous now!
Please, O Hashem, make us prosperous now!

The following four verses are each recited twice:

Blessed be he who has come in the name of Hashem; we bless you from the house of Hashem.
Hashem is God, and He gave us light. Bind the sacrifice with ropes until it is brought to the corners of the altar.
You are my God and I shall thank You; the God of my father, and I shall exalt You.
Give thanks to Hashem because He is good, for His kindness is eternal.

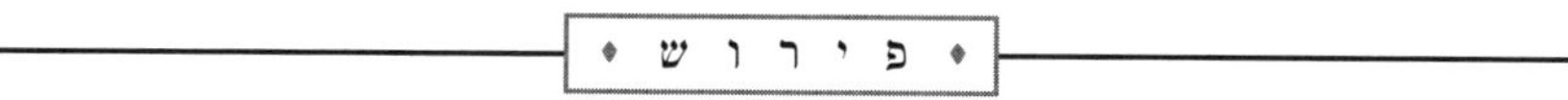

child causes an infringement on his honor. In the sefer, *Ohr Torah,* we find that a father will even allow a baby to pull on his beard.

So too, when we pray to Hashem for mercy from our lowest point, מן המצר, Hashem lowers Himself, as it were, and brings us up to a higher place—to a מרחב.

♦ ♦ ♦ ♦ ♦ ♦

At the time of *Ikvesa D'Meshicha*—the era before Moshiach's arrival—the hatred of the other nations towards the Jewish People will significantly increase. This is because at that time, they will sense that their end is near, and will use all their powers to try and fight the impending end.

הודו לַיְיָ כִּי טוֹב,	כִּי לְעוֹלָם חַסְדּוֹ:
הוֹדוּ לֵאלֹהֵי הָאֱלֹהִים,	כִּי לְעוֹלָם חַסְדּוֹ:
הוֹדוּ לַאֲדֹנֵי הָאֲדֹנִים,	כִּי לְעוֹלָם חַסְדּוֹ:
לְעֹשֵׂה נִפְלָאוֹת גְּדֹלוֹת לְבַדּוֹ,	כִּי לְעוֹלָם חַסְדּוֹ:
לְעֹשֵׂה הַשָּׁמַיִם בִּתְבוּנָה,	כִּי לְעוֹלָם חַסְדּוֹ:
לְרוֹקַע הָאָרֶץ עַל הַמָּיִם,	כִּי לְעוֹלָם חַסְדּוֹ:
לְעֹשֵׂה אוֹרִים גְּדֹלִים,	כִּי לְעוֹלָם חַסְדּוֹ:
אֶת הַשֶּׁמֶשׁ לְמֶמְשֶׁלֶת בַּיּוֹם,	כִּי לְעוֹלָם חַסְדּוֹ:
אֶת הַיָּרֵחַ וְכוֹכָבִים לְמֶמְשְׁלוֹת בַּלָּיְלָה,	כִּי לְעוֹלָם חַסְדּוֹ:

פירוש

When we witness this seething hatred, we should not despair. On the contrary, we should rejoice, for this is the indication that the Moshiach is about to arrive. He is very near, and we should take comfort in the ultimate Day of Judgment our enemies already sense.

This is what we say in Hallel—"ה׳ לי בעוזרי—Hashem is to me, to my help." How do I know this? "ואני אראה בשונאי—and I see it in my enemies." When I see that their hatred is growing stronger, I know that the geulah cannot be far away.

♦ ♦ ♦ ♦ ♦ ♦

אוֹדְךָ כִּי עֲנִיתָנִי

R' Levi Yitzchok of Berditchev in his sefer, *Kedushas Levi*, says that true

Give thanks to Hashem because He is good,
for His kindness is eternal.
Give thanks to the God of the angels,
for His kindness is eternal.
Give thanks to Hashem of Hashems, for His kindness is eternal.
To Him Who performs great wonders alone,
for His kindness is eternal.
To Him Who made the heavens with understanding,
for His kindness is eternal.
To Him Who spread out the earth over the water,
for His kindness is eternal.
To Him Who made great luminaries, for His kindness is eternal.
The sun to rule by day, for His kindness is eternal.
The moon and stars to rule by night, for His kindness is eternal.

♦ פ י ר ו ש ♦

simcha occurs when we acheive something after some difficulty. When something comes easily, the joy is incomplete. In fact, the entire purpose of the difficulty was to provide the *yeshua*.

It says in Tehillim (136:4), "אבן מאסו הבונים היתה לראש פינה—the stone that the builders rejected became the cornerstone." Sometimes what appears to us to be difficult, unpleasant, and even worthy of rejection becomes the foundation for our salvation.

♦ ♦ ♦ ♦ ♦ ♦

לְעֹשֵׂה נִפְלָאוֹת גְּדֹלוֹת לְבַדּוֹ

In some situations, there are no natural means of salvation. Only a miracle, something supernatural, can extricate a person from such a plight.

לְמַכֵּה מִצְרַיִם בִּבְכוֹרֵיהֶם, כִּי לְעוֹלָם חַסְדּוֹ:

וַיּוֹצֵא יִשְׂרָאֵל מִתּוֹכָם, כִּי לְעוֹלָם חַסְדּוֹ:

בְּיָד חֲזָקָה וּבִזְרוֹעַ נְטוּיָה, כִּי לְעוֹלָם חַסְדּוֹ:

לְגֹזֵר יַם סוּף לִגְזָרִים, כִּי לְעוֹלָם חַסְדּוֹ:

וְהֶעֱבִיר יִשְׂרָאֵל בְּתוֹכוֹ, כִּי לְעוֹלָם חַסְדּוֹ:

וְנִעֵר פַּרְעֹה וְחֵילוֹ בְיַם סוּף, כִּי לְעוֹלָם חַסְדּוֹ:

לְמוֹלִיךְ עַמּוֹ בַּמִּדְבָּר, כִּי לְעוֹלָם חַסְדּוֹ:

לְמַכֵּה מְלָכִים גְּדֹלִים, כִּי לְעוֹלָם חַסְדּוֹ:

וַיַּהֲרֹג מְלָכִים אַדִּירִים, כִּי לְעוֹלָם חַסְדּוֹ:

לְסִיחוֹן מֶלֶךְ הָאֱמֹרִי, כִּי לְעוֹלָם חַסְדּוֹ:

וּלְעוֹג מֶלֶךְ הַבָּשָׁן, כִּי לְעוֹלָם חַסְדּוֹ:

וְנָתַן אַרְצָם לְנַחֲלָה, כִּי לְעוֹלָם חַסְדּוֹ:

נַחֲלָה לְיִשְׂרָאֵל עַבְדּוֹ, כִּי לְעוֹלָם חַסְדּוֹ:

♦ פירוש ♦

But miracles are miracles, and one must be worthy.

What if one does not have the merits one needs at such a time? Hakadosh Boruch Hu will perform the נפלאות גדולות—the extraordinary wonders, לבדו—on His own accord, without the person's merit (Toldos Yitzchok).

To Him Who struck the Egyptians with their firstborn,
for His kindness is eternal.

And He took Israel from their midst, for His kindness is eternal.

With a strong hand and with an outstretched arm,
for His kindness is eternal.

To Him Who cut the Sea of Reeds asunder,
for His kindness is eternal.

And caused Israel to cross in its midst,
for His kindness is eternal.

And threw Pharaoh and his army into the Sea of Reeds,
for His kindness is eternal.

To Him Who led His people in the desert,
for His kindness is eternal.

To Him Who struck down great kings,
for His kindness is eternal.

And slew mighty kings, for His kindness is eternal.

Sihon, the king of the Amorites, for His kindness is eternal.

And Og, the king of Bashan, for His kindness is eternal.

And He gave their land as an inheritance,
for His kindness is eternal.

An inheritance to Israel, His servant, for His kindness is eternal.

♦ ♦ ♦ ♦ ♦ ♦

HaGaon HaRav Simcha Wasserman zt"l, Rosh Yeshiva of Ohr Elchanan, offers an insight into miracles.

The Gemarah tells us the story of Rabbi Chaninah ben Dosah. He was so poor he would subsist on a little bit of carob from Erev Shabbos

שֶׁבְּשִׁפְלֵנוּ זָכַר לָנוּ, כִּי לְעוֹלָם חַסְדּוֹ:

וַיִּפְרְקֵנוּ מִצָּרֵינוּ, כִּי לְעוֹלָם חַסְדּוֹ:

נוֹתֵן לֶחֶם לְכָל בָּשָׂר, כִּי לְעוֹלָם חַסְדּוֹ:

הוֹדוּ לְאֵל הַשָּׁמָיִם, כִּי לְעוֹלָם חַסְדּוֹ:

נִשְׁמַת כָּל חַי, תְּבָרֵךְ אֶת שִׁמְךָ יְיָ אֱלֹהֵינוּ. וְרוּחַ כָּל בָּשָׂר, תְּפָאֵר וּתְרוֹמֵם זִכְרְךָ מַלְכֵּנוּ תָּמִיד, מִן הָעוֹלָם וְעַד הָעוֹלָם אַתָּה אֵל. וּמִבַּלְעָדֶיךָ אֵין לָנוּ מֶלֶךְ גּוֹאֵל וּמוֹשִׁיעַ, פּוֹדֶה וּמַצִּיל וּמְפַרְנֵס וּמְרַחֵם, בְּכָל עֵת צָרָה וְצוּקָה. אֵין לָנוּ מֶלֶךְ אֶלָּא אָתָּה: אֱלֹהֵי הָרִאשׁוֹנִים וְהָאַחֲרוֹנִים, אֱלוֹהַ כָּל בְּרִיּוֹת, אֲדוֹן כָּל תּוֹלָדוֹת, הַמְהֻלָּל בְּרֹב הַתִּשְׁבָּחוֹת, הַמְנַהֵג עוֹלָמוֹ בְּחֶסֶד, וּבְרִיּוֹתָיו בְּרַחֲמִים. וַיְיָ לֹא יָנוּם וְלֹא יִישָׁן, הַמְעוֹרֵר יְשֵׁנִים

♦ פירוש ♦

to Erev Shabbos. One Friday evening, when his daughter was preparing the candles for Shabbos, she mistakenly filled the candelabra with vin egar instead of oil. After she tried to light the wicks, she went running to Rabbi Chaninah, distraught, and told him that she couldn't get the candles to burn.

Rabbi Chaninah's faith did not fail him.

"He Who has commanded oil to burn shall command the vinegar to burn." The candles burned as bright as ever.

Why, indeed, does oil burn? What sets oil apart from other liquids that cannot hold fire? The truth is, most of us don't actually know. We have merely become accustomed to the facts of nature, and so, we don't ever even question the marvel of it. But the fact that oil burns is a

Who remembered us in our humble state,
for His kindness is eternal.

And he rescued us from our adversaries,
for His kindness is eternal.

Who gives food to all flesh, for His kindness is eternal.

Give thanks to the God of heaven, for His kindness is eternal.

The soul of every living thing shall praise Your name, Hashem, our God, and the spirit of all flesh shall glorify and forever exalt Your remembrance, our King. From eternity to eternity You are God. Besides You, we have no king Who redeems and saves, ransoms, rescues, sustains and shows mercy. In every time of trouble and distress, we have no king but You. You are God of the first and of the last, God of all creations, Master of all generations, Who is acclaimed with many praises, Who rules His world with kindness and His creatures with mercy. God neither slumbers nor sleeps. He awakens the sleepers

wonder.

And vinegar? Vinegar never burns. But on that Shabbos, in the home of Rabbi Chaninah ben Dosah, ordinary vinegar assumed the power of oil, and burned. That is a miracle.

♦ ♦ ♦ ♦ ♦ ♦

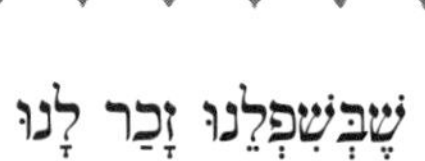

In his sefer, *Degel Machane Ephraim*, Rabbi Moshe Chaim Ephraim, the Tzaddik of Sudilkov, writes שבשפלנו, when we humble ourselves in front of Hashem, then we will merit that the Divine Presence hover over us.

The Mishnah in Pirkei Avos (4:4) says "מאד מאד הוי שפל רוח—a person must be exceedingly humble." Why does one have to be "exceedingly"

וְהַמֵּקִיץ נִרְדָּמִים, וְהַמֵּשִׂיחַ אִלְּמִים, וְהַמַּתִּיר אֲסוּרִים, וְהַסּוֹמֵךְ נוֹפְלִים, וְהַזּוֹקֵף כְּפוּפִים, לְךָ לְבַדְּךָ אֲנַחְנוּ מוֹדִים. אִלּוּ פִינוּ מָלֵא שִׁירָה כַּיָּם, וּלְשׁוֹנֵנוּ רִנָּה כַּהֲמוֹן גַּלָּיו, וְשִׂפְתוֹתֵינוּ שֶׁבַח כְּמֶרְחֲבֵי רָקִיעַ, וְעֵינֵינוּ מְאִירוֹת כַּשֶּׁמֶשׁ וְכַיָּרֵחַ, וְיָדֵינוּ פְרוּשׂוֹת כְּנִשְׁרֵי שָׁמָיִם, וְרַגְלֵינוּ קַלּוֹת כָּאַיָּלוֹת, אֵין אֲנַחְנוּ מַסְפִּיקִים, לְהוֹדוֹת לְךָ יְיָ אֱלֹהֵינוּ וֵאלֹהֵי אֲבוֹתֵינוּ, וּלְבָרֵךְ אֶת שְׁמֶךָ עַל אַחַת מֵאָלֶף אֶלֶף אַלְפֵי אֲלָפִים וְרִבֵּי רְבָבוֹת פְּעָמִים, הַטּוֹבוֹת שֶׁעָשִׂיתָ עִם אֲבוֹתֵינוּ וְעִמָּנוּ. מִמִּצְרַיִם גְּאַלְתָּנוּ יְיָ אֱלֹהֵינוּ, וּמִבֵּית עֲבָדִים פְּדִיתָנוּ, בְּרָעָב זַנְתָּנוּ, וּבְשָׂבָע כִּלְכַּלְתָּנוּ, מֵחֶרֶב הִצַּלְתָּנוּ, וּמִדֶּבֶר מִלַּטְתָּנוּ, וּמֵחֳלָיִם רָעִים וְנֶאֱמָנִים דִּלִּיתָנוּ: עַד הֵנָּה עֲזָרוּנוּ רַחֲמֶיךָ, וְלֹא עֲזָבוּנוּ חֲסָדֶיךָ וְאַל תִּטְּשֵׁנוּ יְיָ אֱלֹהֵינוּ לָנֶצַח. עַל כֵּן אֵבָרִים שֶׁפִּלַּגְתָּ בָּנוּ, וְרוּחַ וּנְשָׁמָה שֶׁנָּפַחְתָּ בְּאַפֵּינוּ, וְלָשׁוֹן אֲשֶׁר שַׂמְתָּ בְּפִינוּ, הֵן הֵם יוֹדוּ וִיבָרְכוּ וִישַׁבְּחוּ וִיפָאֲרוּ וִירוֹמְמוּ וְיַעֲרִיצוּ וְיַקְדִּישׁוּ וְיַמְלִיכוּ אֶת שִׁמְךָ מַלְכֵּנוּ, כִּי כָל פֶּה לְךָ יוֹדֶה, וְכָל לָשׁוֹן לְךָ תִשָּׁבַע, וְכָל בֶּרֶךְ לְךָ תִכְרַע, וְכָל קוֹמָה לְפָנֶיךָ תִשְׁתַּחֲוֶה, וְכָל לְבָבוֹת יִירָאוּךָ, וְכָל קֶרֶב וּכְלָיוֹת יְזַמְּרוּ לִשְׁמֶךָ. כַּדָּבָר שֶׁכָּתוּב, כָּל עַצְמוֹתַי תֹּאמַרְנָה יְיָ מִי כָמוֹךָ. מַצִּיל עָנִי מֵחָזָק מִמֶּנּוּ, וְעָנִי וְאֶבְיוֹן מִגֹּזְלוֹ: מִי יִדְמֶה לָּךְ, וּמִי יִשְׁוֶה לָּךְ וּמִי יַעֲרָךְ לָךְ: הָאֵל הַגָּדוֹל הַגִּבּוֹר וְהַנּוֹרָא, אֵל עֶלְיוֹן קֹנֵה שָׁמַיִם וָאָרֶץ: נְהַלֶּלְךָ וּנְשַׁבֵּחֲךָ וּנְפָאֶרְךָ וּנְבָרֵךְ אֶת שֵׁם קָדְשֶׁךָ. כָּאָמוּר, לְדָוִד, בָּרְכִי נַפְשִׁי אֶת יְיָ, וְכָל קְרָבַי אֶת שֵׁם קָדְשׁוֹ:

and arouses the slumberers, causes the mute to speak, frees the imprisoned, supports the fallen and straightens the bent. To You alone we give thanks. Even if our mouths were filled with song like the sea, our tongues with rejoicing like the multitude of its waves, our lips with praise like the expanse of the heaven, our eyes as radiant as the sun and the moon, our hands as outspread as the eagles in the sky, and our feet as swift as deer, we could never sufficiently praise You, Hashem, our God and the God of our fathers, or bless Your Name for even one of the thousands upon thousands, and myriads upon myriads of the kindnesses that You have done for our fathers and for us. From Egypt You redeemed us, Hashem, our God, and from the house of slavery You released us. In famine You fed us, and in plenty You sustained us. From the sword You saved us, and from pestilence You delivered us , and from harsh and serious illnesses You spared us. Until now, Your mercies have helped us, and Your kindnesses have not forsaken us. Do not abandon us, Hashem our God, forever. Therefore, the limbs that You formed in us, and the breath and spirit that You blew into our nostrils and the tongues that You placed into our mouths—they themselves will thank, bless, praise, glorify, exalt, revere, sanctify and proclaim the sovereignty of Your Name, our King. For every mouth will thank You, every tongue will swear to You, every knee will bend to You, every being that stands will prostrate itself to You, all hearts will fear You, and all innermost parts will sing to Your name. As it is written: "All my bones will say, 'God, who is like You? Who saves the poor man from one that is stronger than him or the poor and the needy from one who wishes to rob him?'" Who is like You? Who is equal to You? Who can be compared to You? The great, mighty, awesome God, lofty God, Creator of heaven and earth. We will praise You, acclaim You, glorify You and bless Your holy name. As it is said: Of David. "Bless, Hashem, O my soul, and all that is within me, bless His holy name."

הָאֵל בְּתַעֲצֻמוֹת עֻזֶּךָ, הַגָּדוֹל בִּכְבוֹד שְׁמֶךָ. הַגִּבּוֹר לָנֶצַח וְהַנּוֹרָא בְּנוֹרְאוֹתֶיךָ. הַמֶּלֶךְ הַיּוֹשֵׁב עַל כִּסֵּא רָם וְנִשָּׂא:

שׁוֹכֵן עַד, מָרוֹם וְקָדוֹשׁ שְׁמוֹ: וְכָתוּב, רַנְּנוּ צַדִּיקִים בַּיְיָ, לַיְשָׁרִים נָאוָה תְהִלָּה. בְּפִי יְשָׁרִים תִּתְהַלָּל. וּבְדִבְרֵי צַדִּיקִים תִּתְבָּרַךְ. וּבִלְשׁוֹן חֲסִידִים תִּתְרוֹמָם. וּבְקֶרֶב קְדוֹשִׁים תִּתְקַדָּשׁ:

וּבְמַקְהֲלוֹת רִבְבוֹת עַמְּךָ בֵּית יִשְׂרָאֵל, בְּרִנָּה יִתְפָּאַר שִׁמְךָ מַלְכֵּנוּ, בְּכָל דּוֹר וָדוֹר, שֶׁכֵּן חוֹבַת כָּל הַיְצוּרִים, לְפָנֶיךָ יְיָ אֱלֹהֵינוּ, וֵאלֹהֵי אֲבוֹתֵינוּ, לְהוֹדוֹת לְהַלֵּל לְשַׁבֵּחַ לְפָאֵר לְרוֹמֵם לְהַדֵּר לְבָרֵךְ לְעַלֵּה וּלְקַלֵּס, עַל כָּל דִּבְרֵי שִׁירוֹת וְתִשְׁבְּחוֹת דָּוִד בֶּן יִשַׁי עַבְדְּךָ מְשִׁיחֶךָ:

יִשְׁתַּבַּח שִׁמְךָ לָעַד מַלְכֵּנוּ, הָאֵל הַמֶּלֶךְ הַגָּדוֹל וְהַקָּדוֹשׁ בַּשָּׁמַיִם וּבָאָרֶץ. כִּי לְךָ נָאֶה, יְיָ אֱלֹהֵינוּ וֵאלֹהֵי אֲבוֹתֵינוּ: שִׁיר וּשְׁבָחָה, הַלֵּל וְזִמְרָה, עֹז וּמֶמְשָׁלָה, נֶצַח, גְּדֻלָּה וּגְבוּרָה, תְּהִלָּה וְתִפְאֶרֶת, קְדֻשָּׁה וּמַלְכוּת. בְּרָכוֹת וְהוֹדָאוֹת מֵעַתָּה וְעַד עוֹלָם.

פירוש

humble? It has been suggested that being humble is such a difficult charge that if one's goal is to be exceedingly humble, one will at least reach some level of humility.

When one of the eminent gedolei mussar R' Yitzchok Blazer (better known as R' Itzele Peterburger) finally was permitted to emigrate to Eretz Yisroel, a huge gathering was convened in his honor shortly after he had arrived. The gathering took place in one of the largest convention halls in Yerushalayim.

All of the people had crowded in and the room was packed to capac-

O God in the strength of Your power. Great in the honor of Your name. Strong forever, and awesome in Your awesome deeds! The King Who sits on a high and lofty throne!

The One Who dwells for eternity, exalted and holy is His name! And it is written: "Rejoice in Hashem, O you righteous, praise is comely to the upright." In the mouths of the upright You will be praised, and in the words of the righteous You will be blessed, and in the tongues of the pious You will be exalted, and in the midst of the holy You will be sanctified.

And in the assemblies of the myriads of Your people, the House of Israel, Your name, our King, will be glorified with song in every generation; for such is the obligation of all creations, Hashem, our God and the God of our fathers, to offer thanks, praise, and tribute, to glorify, exalt, revere, bless, elevate, and adore You, beyond all the words of songs and praises of David, son of Jesse, Your servant, Your anointed one.

May Your name be praised forever, our King, God and King, great and holy in heaven and earth, for to You is befitting, Hashem, our God and God of our fathers, song and praise, acclaim and melody, strength and rulership, victory, greatness and might, praise and glory, holiness and kingship, blessings and thanksgivings, from now and forever.

ity. Everyone was waiting impatiently; it seemed that the guest of honor had still not arrived.

All of a sudden, someone spotted R' Itzele sitting in the very last row. He simply was not interested in being the center of attention.

♦ ♦ ♦ ♦ ♦ ♦

There is a *machlokes* (a difference of opinion) among the sages concern-

יְהַלְלוּךָ יְיָ אֱלֹהֵינוּ כָּל מַעֲשֶׂיךָ, וַחֲסִידֶיךָ צַדִּיקִים עוֹשֵׂי רְצוֹנֶךָ, וְכָל עַמְּךָ בֵּית יִשְׂרָאֵל בְּרִנָּה יוֹדוּ וִיבָרְכוּ וִישַׁבְּחוּ וִיפָאֲרוּ וִירוֹמְמוּ וְיַעֲרִיצוּ וְיַקְדִּישׁוּ וְיַמְלִיכוּ אֶת שִׁמְךָ מַלְכֵּנוּ, כִּי לְךָ טוֹב לְהוֹדוֹת וּלְשִׁמְךָ נָאֶה לְזַמֵּר, כִּי מֵעוֹלָם וְעַד עוֹלָם אַתָּה אֵל. בָּרוּךְ אַתָּה יְיָ, אֵל מֶלֶךְ מְהֻלָּל בַּתִּשְׁבָּחוֹת.

While reclining on our left side, we raise the cup of wine, recite the following blessing and drink the fourth cup of wine.

בָּרוּךְ אַתָּה יְיָ, אֱלֹהֵינוּ מֶלֶךְ הָעוֹלָם, בּוֹרֵא פְּרִי הַגָּפֶן:

We now recite the following, adding the sentence in brackets on Shabbos:

בָּרוּךְ אַתָּה יְיָ אֱלֹהֵינוּ מֶלֶךְ הָעוֹלָם עַל הַגֶּפֶן וְעַל פְּרִי הַגֶּפֶן וְעַל תְּנוּבַת הַשָּׂדֶה, וְעַל אֶרֶץ חֶמְדָּה טוֹבָה וּרְחָבָה, שֶׁרָצִיתָ וְהִנְחַלְתָּ לַאֲבוֹתֵינוּ, לֶאֱכוֹל מִפִּרְיָהּ וְלִשְׂבּוֹעַ מִטּוּבָהּ. רַחֵם נָא יְיָ אֱלֹהֵינוּ עַל יִשְׂרָאֵל עַמֶּךָ, וְעַל יְרוּשָׁלַיִם עִירֶךָ, וְעַל צִיּוֹן מִשְׁכַּן

♦ פירוש ♦

ing the construction of the third Bais Hamikdash. The Rambam states in *Mishneh Torah*, (*Hilchos Melochim* 11:1, 4) that the Bais Hamikdash will be built by man. In fact, he states, it will be built by Moshiach. Therefore, one of the signs of Moshiach's arrival will be the construction of the Bais Hamikdash.

Rashi, in *Mesechta Succah* 41a and *Rosh Hashanah* 30a explains that Hashem has already built the Bais Hamikdash and it is in existence in the Heavenly spheres. It awaits the time when it will descend to the earthly world. As we say, the third Bais Hamikdash is Hashem's sanctuary, "established by Your Hand" (Shemos 15:17). When the correct moment arrives, the Bais Hamikdash will descend and become part of our world.

All Your works will praise You, Hashem, our God, and Your pious ones, the righteous who perform Your will, and all Your people, the house of Israel, will joyously give thanks, bless, praise, glorify, extol, exalt, revere, sanctify, and crown Your name, our King, for it is good to thank You, and it is fitting to sing to Your name, for from everlasting to everlasting, You are God. Blessed are You, Hashem, King acclaimed with praises.

While reclining on our left side, we raise the cup of wine, recite the following blessing and drink the fourth cup of wine.

Blessed are You, Hashem, our God, King of the universe, Who created the fruit of the vine.

We now recite the following, adding the sentence in brackets on Shabbos:

Blessed are You, Hashem our God, King of the universe, for the vine and for the fruit of the vine and for the produce of the field, and for the desirable, good, and spacious land, which You were pleased to give as a heritage to our forefathers, to eat of its fruit and to become satisfied from its goodness. Have mercy, Hashem, our God, upon Israel Your people, upon Jerusalem Your city, upon Mount Zion the dwelling place of

Our chachomim tell us that in the era of R' Yehoshua ben Chananya, the Romans granted the Jews permission to rebuild the Bais Hamikdash. However, although the people rushed to begin the preparations, the project never got off the ground because of the Samaritans' intervention.

We find an interesting discussion in the Gemarah in which R' Nachman bar Yitzchok says that those who bring joy to a chosson and kallah it is as if they have rebuilt one of the ruins of Yerushalayim (Brochos 6:2).

An interesting question arises: What is the connection between a chosson and kallah and Yerushalayim's ruins?

We learn in Parshas Vayigash that Yosef fell upon Binyomin's neck

כְּבוֹדֶךָ, וְעַל מִזְבְּחֶךָ וְעַל הֵיכָלֶךָ. וּבְנֵה יְרוּשָׁלַיִם עִיר הַקֹּדֶשׁ בִּמְהֵרָה בְיָמֵינוּ, וְהַעֲלֵנוּ לְתוֹכָהּ, וְשַׂמְּחֵנוּ בְּבִנְיָנָהּ וְנֹאכַל מִפִּרְיָהּ וְנִשְׂבַּע מִטּוּבָהּ, וּנְבָרֶכְךָ עָלֶיהָ בִּקְדֻשָּׁה וּבְטָהֳרָה (וּרְצֵה וְהַחֲלִיצֵנוּ בְּיוֹם הַשַּׁבָּת הַזֶּה) וְשַׂמְּחֵנוּ בְּיוֹם חַג הַמַּצּוֹת הַזֶּה. כִּי אַתָּה יְיָ טוֹב וּמֵטִיב לַכֹּל, וְנוֹדֶה לְּךָ עַל הָאָרֶץ וְעַל פְּרִי הַגָּפֶן. בָּרוּךְ אַתָּה יְיָ, עַל הָאָרֶץ וְעַל פְּרִי הַגָּפֶן:

פירוש

and Binyomin fell upon Yosef's neck. Rashi explains that they cried about both *Botei Mikdosh* that would be destroyed in the future. It seems strange that at a moment of such great emotion, when beloved brothers were meeting after twenty-two years of separation, they found it proper to cry about what would happen many years in the future.

The brothers realized that the many *yesurim* their *mishpocho* had experienced over the twenty-two years, including their father who could not be comforted, and the Shechinah being sent into exile, all had been caused by the brother's baseless hatred towards Yosef. This is precisely why, at this moment, they cried over the destruction of the Bais Hamikdash that also came about because of baseless hatred. This crying allowed them to accept each other's pain and increase their love for each other. That love atoned for the baseless hatred.

Therefore we can understand why a person bringing joy to a chosson and kallah is as if they have rebuilt one of Yerushalayim's ruins. Through causing a chosson and kallah to rejoice—an act of true ahavas Yisroel—we merit to build one the Bais Hamikdash's fallen ruins, which was destroyed because of שנאת חנם.

♦ ♦ ♦ ♦ ♦ ♦

נִרְצָה

Rabbi Yissocher Dov of Belz points out that one of the reasons we conclude the seder with the word נרצה is because it has the same gematriya as the word משה, to indicate that all that we have done at the seder is

Your glory, upon Your altar, and upon Your Temple. Rebuild Jerusalem the holy city, quickly in our days. Bring us up there and make us happy in its rebuilding. Let us eat of its fruit and become satisfied from its goodness. And we will bless You for it, in holiness and purity. [And may it be acceptable to You, that You strengthen us on this Shabbos day,] and cause us to rejoice on this holiday of matzos. For You, O Hashem, are good and kind to all, and we thank You for the land and the fruit of the vine. Blessed are You, Hashem, for the land and for the fruit of the vine.

♦ פירוש ♦

halacha l'moshe m'sinai.

Once, in the 18th century, there was someone who ridiculed and made fun of the song "chad gadya." One of the rabbis present was so upset and disturbed by this that he placed the man in cherem. The people present later asked the Chidah (Rav Chaim Dovid Azulai), "Did the man deserve such harsh treatment and was the ban legal?" The Chidah responded that the holy Arizal maintained that the songs sung during the Seder were based on deep Kabbalistic foundations that could be traced back to Sinai. He concluded that the man should certainly have been placed in cherem. However, it behooved the rabbi to explain to the man the severity of his sin. The man should be instructed to do teshuva and then the cherem should be lifted.

We see from this that all valid expressions in the service of Hashem are sacred, even if they may not be our own personal custom. In Tehillim 150 we say, "praise Hashem with the shofar... with the lyre... the harp, praise Him with drums and dance... organ and flute... cymbals and trumpets."

This alludes to how each of us approaches Hashem from slightly different points on the spectrum, with different traditions and customs. We all employ our own particular "instruments" to serve Hashem. Although the these tools may vary, the end result is that they all join together in beautiful harmony in praise of Hashem.

This is reflected by the very last line of Tehillim: "let all neshamos praise Hashem."

♦ ♦ ♦ ♦ ♦ ♦

נִרְצָה

חֲסַל סִדּוּר פֶּסַח כְּהִלְכָתוֹ, כְּכָל מִשְׁפָּטוֹ וְחֻקָּתוֹ. כַּאֲשֶׁר זָכִינוּ לְסַדֵּר אוֹתוֹ, כֵּן נִזְכֶּה לַעֲשׂוֹתוֹ. זָךְ שׁוֹכֵן מְעוֹנָה, קוֹמֵם קְהַל עֲדַת מִי מָנָה. בְּקָרוֹב נַהֵל נִטְעֵי כַנָּה, פְּדוּיִם לְצִיּוֹן בְּרִנָּה.

לְשָׁנָה הַבָּאָה בִּירוּשָׁלָיִם!

The following is said only on the first night of the Seder.
On the second night, turn to page 138.

וּבְכֵן וַיְהִי בַּחֲצִי הַלַּיְלָה.

אָז רוֹב נִסִּים הִפְלֵאתָ בַּלַּיְלָה,
בְּרֹאשׁ אַשְׁמוּרוֹת זֶה הַלַּיְלָה,
גֵּר צֶדֶק נִצַּחְתּוֹ כְּנֶחֱלַק לוֹ לַיְלָה,
וַיְהִי בַּחֲצִי הַלַּיְלָה.

דַּנְתָּ מֶלֶךְ גְּרָר בַּחֲלוֹם הַלַּיְלָה,
הִפְחַדְתָּ אֲרַמִּי בְּאֶמֶשׁ לַיְלָה,
וַיָּשַׂר יִשְׂרָאֵל לְמַלְאָךְ וַיּוּכַל לוֹ לַיְלָה,
וַיְהִי בַּחֲצִי הַלַּיְלָה.

זֶרַע בְּכוֹרֵי פַתְרוֹס מָחַצְתָּ בַּחֲצִי הַלַּיְלָה,
חֵילָם לֹא מָצְאוּ בְּקוּמָם בַּלַּיְלָה,
טִיסַת נְגִיד חֲרֹשֶׁת סִלִּיתָ בְכוֹכְבֵי לַיְלָה,
וַיְהִי בַּחֲצִי הַלַּיְלָה.

Nirtzah

The Pesach service is now completed in accordance with its laws, according to all its regulations and statutes. Just as we have been privileged to arrange it, so may we be privileged to perform it. O Pure One Who dwells in heaven, raise up the assembly of Your innumerable people. Quickly, guide the offshoots of Your stock, redeemed to Zion with joyous song.

Next Year in Jerusalem!

The following is said only on the first night of the Seder.
On the second night, turn to page 139.

And so it came to pass at midnight.

Previously, You performed many miracles at night.
At the start of the watch of this night
You caused the righteous convert (Abraham)
to be victorious when he divided (his camp) at night.
It came to pass at midnight.

You judged the king of Gerar (Abimelech) in a dream at night.
You frightened (Laban) the Aramean in the night.
And Israel wrestled with the angel and overcame him at night.
It came to pass at midnight.

You destroyed the firstborn of the Egyptians
in the dark of the night.
They did not find their wealth when they arose at night.
The army of the prince of Charosheth (Sisera)
You swept away with the stars of night.
It came to pass at midnight.

יָעַץ מְחָרֵף לְנוֹפֵף אִוּוּי, הוֹבַשְׁתָּ פְגָרָיו בַּלַּיְלָה,
כָּרַע בֵּל וּמַצָּבוֹ בְּאִישׁוֹן לַיְלָה,
לְאִישׁ חֲמוּדוֹת נִגְלָה רָז חֲזוֹת לַיְלָה,
וַיְהִי בַּחֲצִי הַלַּיְלָה.

מִשְׁתַּכֵּר בִּכְלֵי קֹדֶשׁ נֶהֱרַג בּוֹ בַּלַּיְלָה,
נוֹשַׁע מִבּוֹר אֲרָיוֹת פּוֹתֵר בִּעֲתוּתֵי לַיְלָה.
שִׂנְאָה נָטַר אֲגָגִי וְכָתַב סְפָרִים לַיְלָה,
וַיְהִי בַּחֲצִי הַלַּיְלָה.

עוֹרַרְתָּ נִצְחֲךָ עָלָיו בְּנֶדֶד שְׁנַת לַיְלָה,
פּוּרָה תִדְרוֹךְ לְשׁוֹמֵר מַה מִּלַּיְלָה,
צָרַח כַּשּׁוֹמֵר וְשָׂח אָתָא בֹקֶר וְגַם לַיְלָה,
וַיְהִי בַּחֲצִי הַלַּיְלָה.

קָרֵב יוֹם אֲשֶׁר הוּא לֹא יוֹם וְלֹא לַיְלָה,
רָם הוֹדַע כִּי לְךָ הַיּוֹם אַף לְךָ הַלַּיְלָה,
שׁוֹמְרִים הַפְקֵד לְעִירְךָ כָּל הַיּוֹם וְכָל הַלַּיְלָה,
תָּאִיר כְּאוֹר יוֹם חֶשְׁכַת לַיְלָה,
וַיְהִי בַּחֲצִי הַלַּיְלָה:

◆ פ י ר ו ש ◆

קָרֵב יוֹם אֲשֶׁר הוּא לֹא יוֹם וְלֹא לַיְלָה

When is this day "that is neither day nor night"? Rabbi Chaim Meir of Vizhnitz notes in *Imrei Chaim* that this is Shabbos. On Shabbos, Jews say in greeting neither "good morning" nor "good evening." Instead, on

When the blasphemer (Sancherib) thought to assail Your Temple, You frustrated him with the corpses (of his army) at night.
Bel and his pedestal were humbled in the darkness of night.
To the man of Your favor (Daniel) the secret vision was revealed at night.
It came to pass at midnight.

He who became drunk (Belshazzer) from the holy vessels was killed at night.
He who was saved from the den of lions (Daniel) interpreted the frightening dreams of the night.
The Agagite (Haman) bore hatred and wrote letters at night.
It came to pass at midnight.

You awakened Your victory over him (Haman) when You disturbed (the king's) sleep at night.
You will tread the wine-press for those who ask the watchman "What of the long night?"
He will shout like a watchman and say, "Morning has come, just as night."
It came to pass at midnight.

Bring near the day which is neither day nor night.
O Exalted One! Make known that Yours is the day as well as the night.
Appoint watchmen for Your city, all day and all night.
Illuminate as the light of day, the darkness of night.
It came to pass at midnight.

♦ פירוש ♦

Shabbos, throughout the day and night we simply say "Gut Shabbos."

When Moshiach arrives, Jews will no longer say "good morning" or "good evening." We will always say "Gut Shabbos," both on Shabbos, and during the week, for it will be a time that is "*Yom Shekulo Shabbos*"—"a day that is completely Shabbos."

The following is said only on the second night of the Seder.

וּבְכֵן וַאֲמַרְתֶּם זֶבַח פֶּסַח.

אֹמֶץ גְּבוּרוֹתֶיךָ הִפְלֵאתָ בַּפֶּסַח,
בְּרֹאשׁ כָּל מוֹעֲדוֹת נִשֵּׂאתָ פֶּסַח,
גִּלִּיתָ לְאֶזְרָחִי חֲצוֹת לֵיל פֶּסַח,
וַאֲמַרְתֶּם זֶבַח פֶּסַח.

דְּלָתָיו דָּפַקְתָּ כְּחֹם הַיּוֹם בַּפֶּסַח,
הִסְעִיד נוֹצְצִים עֻגוֹת מַצּוֹת בַּפֶּסַח,
וְאֶל הַבָּקָר רָץ זֵכֶר לְשׁוֹר עֵרֶךְ פֶּסַח,
וַאֲמַרְתֶּם זֶבַח פֶּסַח.

זֹעֲמוּ סְדוֹמִים וְלֹהֲטוּ בָּאֵשׁ בַּפֶּסַח,
חֻלַּץ לוֹט מֵהֶם, וּמַצּוֹת אָפָה בְּקֵץ פֶּסַח,
טִאטֵאתָ אַדְמַת מֹף וְנֹף בְּעָבְרְךָ בַּפֶּסַח,
וַאֲמַרְתֶּם זֶבַח פֶּסַח.

יָהּ, רֹאשׁ כָּל אוֹן מָחַצְתָּ בְּלֵיל שִׁמּוּר פֶּסַח,
כַּבִּיר, עַל בֵּן בְּכוֹר פָּסַחְתָּ בְּדַם פֶּסַח,
לְבִלְתִּי תֵּת מַשְׁחִית לָבֹא בִפְתָחַי בַּפֶּסַח,
וַאֲמַרְתֶּם זֶבַח פֶּסַח.

מְסֻגֶּרֶת סֻגָּרָה בְּעִתּוֹתֵי פֶּסַח,
נִשְׁמְדָה מִדְיָן בִּצְלִיל שְׂעוֹרֵי עֹמֶר פֶּסַח,
שֹׂרְפוּ מִשְׁמַנֵּי פּוּל וְלוּד בִּיקַד יְקוֹד פֶּסַח,
וַאֲמַרְתֶּם זֶבַח פֶּסַח.

The following is said only on the second night of the Seder.

And you shall say: "This is the sacrifice of Pesach."

You demonstrated the strength of Your power on Pesach.
Above all festivals You raised Pesach.
You revealed to Abraham what would
happen at midnight on Pesach.
And you shall say: "This is the sacrifice of Pesach."

You knocked at Abraham's door in
the heat of the day on Pesach.
He fed angels with matzos on Pesach
and he ran to the cattle, in remembrance
of the sacrificial ox of Pesach.
And you shall say: "This is the sacrifice of Pesach."

The Sodomites enraged God and
were destroyed by fire on Pesach.
Lot was separated from them and
baked Matzos at the start of Pesach.
You swept clean the land of Mof and Nof
(in Egypt) when you passed through it on Pesach.
And you shall say: "This is the sacrifice of Pesach."

You, God, destroyed each firstborn
on the watchful night of Pesach.
Mighty One! You passed over Your own firstborn,
because of the blood of the sacrifice of Pesach,
not allowing the destroyer to enter my doors on Pesach.
And you shall say: "This is the sacrifice of Pesach."

The walled city of Jericho was besieged on Pesach.
Midian was destroyed by a cake of barley,
the offering of the Omer on Pesach.
The chiefs of Pul and Lud were burned
in a great fire on Pesach.
And you shall say: "This is the sacrifice of Pesach."

עוֹד הַיּוֹם בְּנֹב לַעֲמוֹד, עַד גָּעָה עוֹנַת פֶּסַח,
פַּס יָד כָּתְבָה לְקַעֲקֵעַ צוּל בַּפֶּסַח,
צָפֹה הַצָּפִית עָרוֹךְ הַשֻּׁלְחָן, בַּפֶּסַח,
וַאֲמַרְתֶּם זֶבַח פֶּסַח.

קָהָל כִּנְּסָה הֲדַסָּה צוֹם לְשַׁלֵּשׁ בַּפֶּסַח,
רֹאשׁ מִבֵּית רָשָׁע מָחַצְתָּ בְּעֵץ חֲמִשִּׁים בַּפֶּסַח,
שְׁתֵּי אֵלֶּה רֶגַע, תָּבִיא לְעוּצִית בַּפֶּסַח,
תָּעֹז יָדְךָ וְתָרוּם יְמִינְךָ, כְּלֵיל הִתְקַדֵּשׁ חַג פֶּסַח,
וַאֲמַרְתֶּם זֶבַח פֶּסַח.

On both nights continue here:

כִּי לוֹ נָאֶה, כִּי לוֹ יָאֶה.

אַדִּיר בִּמְלוּכָה, בָּחוּר כַּהֲלָכָה, גְּדוּדָיו יֹאמְרוּ לוֹ: לְךָ וּלְךָ, לְךָ כִּי לְךָ, לְךָ אַף לְךָ, לְךָ יְיָ הַמַּמְלָכָה. כִּי לוֹ נָאֶה, כִּי לוֹ יָאֶה.

דָּגוּל בִּמְלוּכָה, הָדוּר כַּהֲלָכָה, וָתִיקָיו יֹאמְרוּ לוֹ: לְךָ וּלְךָ, לְךָ כִּי לְךָ, לְךָ אַף לְךָ, לְךָ יְיָ הַמַּמְלָכָה. כִּי לוֹ נָאֶה, כִּי לוֹ יָאֶה.

זַכַּאי בִּמְלוּכָה, חָסִין כַּהֲלָכָה, טַפְסְרָיו יֹאמְרוּ לוֹ: לְךָ וּלְךָ, לְךָ כִּי לְךָ, לְךָ אַף לְךָ, לְךָ יְיָ הַמַּמְלָכָה. כִּי לוֹ נָאֶה, כִּי לוֹ יָאֶה.

יָחִיד בִּמְלוּכָה, כַּבִּיר כַּהֲלָכָה, לִמּוּדָיו יֹאמְרוּ לוֹ: לְךָ וּלְךָ, לְךָ כִּי לְךָ, לְךָ אַף לְךָ, לְךָ יְיָ הַמַּמְלָכָה. כִּי לוֹ נָאֶה, כִּי לוֹ יָאֶה.

He (Sancherib) intended to be that day in Nob,
and wait for the coming of Pesach.
A hand wrote the fate of Zul (Babylon) on Pesach,
just when the watch was set and
the table was spread on Pesach.
And you shall say: "This is the sacrifice of Pesach."

Hadassah (Esther) assembled the congregation
for a three-day fast on Pesach.
The head of the evil house (Haman),
You hung on a fifty-cubit gallows on Pesach.
These two misfortunes You shall suddenly
bring upon Utzith (Edom) on Pesach.
May Your hand be strong, and Your right arm uplifted,
as on the night when You sanctified the festival of Pesach.
And you shall say: "This is the sacrifice of Pesach."

On both nights continue here:

To Him praise is becoming! To Him praise is fitting!

Mighty in kingship, truly chosen. His hosts of angels say to Him: "To You and to You, To You, indeed to You, To You, certainly to You. To You, God, is the sovereignty." To Him praise is becoming! To Him praise is fitting!

Foremost in kingship, truly glorious, His worthy ones say to Him: "To You and to You, To You, indeed to You, To You, certainly to You. To You, God, is the sovereignty." To Him praise is becoming! To Him praise is fitting!

Faultless in kingship, truly strong, His angels say to Him: "To You and to You, To You, indeed to You, To You, certainly to You. To You, God, is the sovereignty." To Him praise is becoming! To Him praise is fitting!

Unique in kingship, truly mighty, His disciples say to Him: "To You and to You, To You, indeed to You, To You, certainly to You. To You, God, is the sovereignty." To Him praise is becoming! To Him praise is fitting!

מוֹשֵׁל בִּמְלוּכָה, נוֹרָא כַּהֲלָכָה, סְבִיבָיו יֹאמְרוּ לוֹ: לְךָ וּלְךָ, לְךָ כִּי לְךָ, לְךָ אַף לְךָ, לְךָ יְיָ הַמַּמְלָכָה. כִּי לוֹ נָאֶה, כִּי לוֹ יָאֶה.

עָנָו בִּמְלוּכָה, פּוֹדֶה כַּהֲלָכָה, צַדִּיקָיו יֹאמְרוּ לוֹ: לְךָ וּלְךָ, לְךָ כִּי לְךָ, לְךָ אַף לְךָ, לְךָ יְיָ הַמַּמְלָכָה. כִּי לוֹ נָאֶה, כִּי לוֹ יָאֶה.

קָדוֹשׁ בִּמְלוּכָה, רַחוּם כַּהֲלָכָה, שִׁנְאַנָּיו יֹאמְרוּ לוֹ: לְךָ וּלְךָ, לְךָ כִּי לְךָ, לְךָ אַף לְךָ, לְךָ יְיָ הַמַּמְלָכָה. כִּי לוֹ נָאֶה, כִּי לוֹ יָאֶה.

תַּקִּיף בִּמְלוּכָה, תּוֹמֵךְ כַּהֲלָכָה, תְּמִימָיו יֹאמְרוּ לוֹ: לְךָ וּלְךָ, לְךָ כִּי לְךָ, לְךָ אַף לְךָ, לְךָ יְיָ הַמַּמְלָכָה. כִּי לוֹ נָאֶה, כִּי לוֹ יָאֶה.

אַדִּיר הוּא, יִבְנֶה בֵיתוֹ בְּקָרוֹב, בִּמְהֵרָה בִּמְהֵרָה, בְּיָמֵינוּ בְּקָרוֹב. אֵל בְּנֵה, בְּנֵה בֵיתְךָ בְּקָרוֹב.

בָּחוּר הוּא, גָּדוֹל הוּא, דָּגוּל הוּא, יִבְנֶה בֵיתוֹ בְּקָרוֹב, בִּמְהֵרָה בִּמְהֵרָה, בְּיָמֵינוּ בְקָרוֹב. אֵל בְּנֵה, אֵל בְּנֵה, בְּנֵה בֵיתְךָ בְּקָרוֹב.

הָדוּר הוּא, וָתִיק הוּא, זַכַּאי הוּא, חָסִיד הוּא, יִבְנֶה בֵיתוֹ בְּקָרוֹב, בִּמְהֵרָה בִּמְהֵרָה, בְּיָמֵינוּ בְקָרוֹב. אֵל בְּנֵה, אֵל בְּנֵה, בְּנֵה בֵיתְךָ בְּקָרוֹב.

Royal in kingship, truly awesome, those around Him say to Him: "To You and to You, To You, indeed to You, To You, certainly to You. To You, God, is the sovereignty." To Him praise is becoming! To Him praise is fitting!

Humble in kingship, truly the redeemer, His righteous ones say to Him: "To You and to You, To You, indeed to You, To You, certainly to You. To You, God, is the sovereignty." To Him praise is becoming! To Him praise is fitting!

Holy in kingship, truly merciful, His angels say to Him: "To You and to You, To You indeed to You, To You certainly to You. To You, God, is the sovereignty" To Him praise is becoming! To Him praise is fitting!

Powerful in kingship, truly sustaining, His perfect ones say to Him: "To You and to You, To You, indeed to You, To You, certainly to You. To You, God, is the sovereignty." To Him praise is becoming! To Him praise is fitting!

Mighty is He. May He rebuild His house soon. Quickly, quickly, in our days soon. God rebuild, God rebuild. Rebuild your House soon!

Chosen is He. Great is He. Foremost is He. May He rebuild His house soon. Quickly, quickly, in our days soon. God rebuild, God rebuild. Rebuild your House soon!

Glorious is He. Worthy is He. Faultless is He. Pious is He. May He rebuild His house soon. Quickly, quickly, in our days soon. God rebuild, God rebuild. Rebuild your House soon!

טָהוֹר הוּא, יָחִיד הוּא, כַּבִּיר הוּא, לָמוּד הוּא, מֶלֶךְ הוּא, נוֹרָא הוּא, סַגִּיב הוּא, עִזּוּז הוּא, פּוֹדֶה הוּא, צַדִּיק הוּא, יִבְנֶה בֵיתוֹ בְּקָרוֹב, בִּמְהֵרָה בִּמְהֵרָה, בְּיָמֵינוּ בְקָרוֹב. אֵל בְּנֵה, אֵל בְּנֵה, בְּנֵה בֵיתְךָ בְּקָרוֹב.

קָדוֹשׁ הוּא, רַחוּם הוּא, שַׁדַּי הוּא, תַּקִּיף הוּא, יִבְנֶה בֵיתוֹ בְּקָרוֹב, בִּמְהֵרָה בִּמְהֵרָה, בְּיָמֵינוּ בְקָרוֹב. אֵל בְּנֵה, אֵל בְּנֵה, בְּנֵה בֵיתְךָ בְּקָרוֹב.

◆ פ י ר ו ש ◆

אֵ-ל בְּנֵה, בְּנֵה

We repeat the words, much as a child repeats his requests to his mother again and again, pleading, begging Hashem to build His House soon.

The third Beis Hamikdash will encompass both the first Beis Hamikdash and the second. Our words reflect this. א-ל בנה—Hashem, rebuild the first Beis Hamikdash; א-ל בנה—Hashem, rebuild the second Beis Hamikdash; בנה ביתך בקרוב—build Your House, the third Beis Hamikdash, that will truly be Your House, very soon.

◆ ◆ ◆ ◆ ◆ ◆

A Belzer chassid was about to travel to Eretz Yisroel. Before his trip, he visited the Belzer Rebbe.

"When you visit the Kosel, count how many stones there are in the wall," said the Rebbe. The chassid did as he was told. When he returned to the Rebbe after his trip, the first thing the Rebbe asked was how many stones there are in the Wall. The chassid told the Rebbe the number.

"You missed one stone," said the Rebbe. The chassid, who had gone to great lengths to get an accurate count, grasped immediately that he had not missed a stone for naught. Rather, he had not been worthy of seeing the particular stone the Rebbe had in mind. He left the Rebbe and began to do teshuva, analyzing his deeds, and praying for forgiveness.

Some time later, he visited the Kosel again. This time, he counted

Pure is He. Unique is He. Mighty is He. Wise is He. King is He. Awesome is He. Exalted is He. Strong is He. Redeemer is He. Righteous is He. May He rebuild His house soon. Quickly, quickly, in our days soon. God rebuild, God rebuild. Rebuild your House soon!

Holy is He. Merciful is He. Almighty is He. Powerful is He. May He rebuild His house soon. Quickly, quickly, in our days soon. God rebuild, God rebuild. Rebuild your House soon!

◆ פ י ר ו ש ◆

the stones ever so carefully and discovered one additional stone!

Elated, he went to the Rebbe as soon as he returned home, and told him that he had counted the missing stone.

"This stone is an extraordinary stone," said the Rebbe. "This stone, that is at first נעלם מהעין—hidden from the eye, is the stone that elevates all of the prayers to the Heavens!"

Let us hope that Jews throughout the world will merit to find the hidden stone, the opening to the Gates of Mercy. May Hakadosh Baruch Hu accept all of our prayers, and send us the salvation we seek, so that we will be able to sing a שיר חדש—a new song, on our redemption, and on the redemption of our spirits.

◆ ◆ ◆ ◆ ◆ ◆

אֶחָד מִי יוֹדֵעַ?

R' Yitzchak Meir Alter, the first Gerrer Rebbe, in his classic Torah commentary, *Chiddushei Harim,* asked: Why do we begin the song of numbers from number one? What's the point of working our way all the way up? If we started at thirteen, and sang the song of thirteen, all of the numbers would be enumerated going backward until one.

We start at one, he says, to demonstrate the path to *avodas* Hashem. We cannot start at the top. We must begin at the very beginning, and work our way up, from the simple to the complex.

אֶחָד מִי יוֹדֵעַ? אֶחָד אֲנִי יוֹדֵעַ: אֶחָד אֱלֹהֵינוּ שֶׁבַּשָּׁמַיִם וּבָאָרֶץ.

שְׁנַיִם מִי יוֹדֵעַ? שְׁנַיִם אֲנִי יוֹדֵעַ: שְׁנֵי לֻחוֹת הַבְּרִית, אֶחָד אֱלֹהֵינוּ שֶׁבַּשָּׁמַיִם וּבָאָרֶץ.

שְׁלֹשָׁה מִי יוֹדֵעַ? שְׁלֹשָׁה אֲנִי יוֹדֵעַ: שְׁלֹשָׁה אָבוֹת, שְׁנֵי לֻחוֹת הַבְּרִית, אֶחָד אֱלֹהֵינוּ שֶׁבַּשָּׁמַיִם וּבָאָרֶץ.

אַרְבַּע מִי יוֹדֵעַ? אַרְבַּע אֲנִי יוֹדֵעַ: אַרְבַּע אִמָּהוֹת, שְׁלֹשָׁה אָבוֹת, שְׁנֵי לֻחוֹת הַבְּרִית, אֶחָד אֱלֹהֵינוּ שֶׁבַּשָּׁמַיִם וּבָאָרֶץ.

חֲמִשָּׁה מִי יוֹדֵעַ? חֲמִשָּׁה אֲנִי יוֹדֵעַ: חֲמִשָּׁה חוּמְשֵׁי תוֹרָה, אַרְבַּע אִמָּהוֹת, שְׁלֹשָׁה אָבוֹת, שְׁנֵי לֻחוֹת הַבְּרִית, אֶחָד אֱלֹהֵינוּ שֶׁבַּשָּׁמַיִם וּבָאָרֶץ.

שִׁשָּׁה מִי יוֹדֵעַ? שִׁשָּׁה אֲנִי יוֹדֵעַ: שִׁשָּׁה סִדְרֵי מִשְׁנָה, חֲמִשָּׁה חוּמְשֵׁי תוֹרָה, אַרְבַּע אִמָּהוֹת, שְׁלֹשָׁה אָבוֹת, שְׁנֵי לֻחוֹת הַבְּרִית, אֶחָד אֱלֹהֵינוּ שֶׁבַּשָּׁמַיִם וּבָאָרֶץ.

שִׁבְעָה מִי יוֹדֵעַ? שִׁבְעָה אֲנִי יוֹדֵעַ: שִׁבְעָה יְמֵי שַׁבַּתָּא, שִׁשָּׁה סִדְרֵי מִשְׁנָה, חֲמִשָּׁה חוּמְשֵׁי תוֹרָה, אַרְבַּע אִמָּהוֹת, שְׁלֹשָׁה אָבוֹת, שְׁנֵי לֻחוֹת הַבְּרִית, אֶחָד אֱלֹהֵינוּ שֶׁבַּשָּׁמַיִם וּבָאָרֶץ.

שְׁמוֹנָה מִי יוֹדֵעַ? שְׁמוֹנָה אֲנִי יוֹדֵעַ: שְׁמוֹנָה יְמֵי מִילָה, שִׁבְעָה יְמֵי שַׁבַּתָּא, שִׁשָּׁה סִדְרֵי מִשְׁנָה, חֲמִשָּׁה חוּמְשֵׁי תוֹרָה, אַרְבַּע אִמָּהוֹת, שְׁלֹשָׁה אָבוֹת, שְׁנֵי לֻחוֹת הַבְּרִית, אֶחָד אֱלֹהֵינוּ שֶׁבַּשָּׁמַיִם וּבָאָרֶץ.

Who knows one? I know one! One is our God in heaven and on earth.

Who knows two? I know two! Two are the Tablets of the Covenant. One is our God in heaven and on earth.
Who knows three? I know three! Three are the Patriarchs. Two are the Tablets of the Covenant. One is our God in heaven and on earth.

Who knows four? I know four! Four are the Matriarchs. Three are the Patriarchs. Two are the Tablets of the Covenant. One is our God in heaven and on earth.

Who knows five? I know five! Five are the books of the Torah. Four are the Matriarchs. Three are the Patriarchs. Two are the Tablets of the Covenant. One is our God in heaven and on earth.

Who knows six? I know six! Six are the orders of the Mishnah. Five are the books of the Torah. Four are the Matriarchs. Three are the Patriarchs. Two are the Tablets of the Covenant. One is our God in heaven and on earth.

Who knows seven? I know seven! Seven are the days of the week. Six are the orders of the Mishnah. Five are the books of the Torah. Four are the Matriarchs. Three are the Patriarchs. Two are the Tablets of the Covenant. One is our God in heaven and on earth.

Who knows eight? I know eight! Eight are the days for circumcision. Seven are the days of the week. Six are the orders of the Mishnah. Five are the books of the Torah. Four are the Matriarchs. Three are the Patriarchs. Two are the Tablets of the Covenant. One is our God in heaven and on earth.

תִּשְׁעָה מִי יוֹדֵעַ? תִּשְׁעָה אֲנִי יוֹדֵעַ: תִּשְׁעָה יַרְחֵי לֵדָה, שְׁמוֹנָה יְמֵי מִילָה, שִׁבְעָה יְמֵי שַׁבַּתָּא, שִׁשָּׁה סִדְרֵי מִשְׁנָה, חֲמִשָּׁה חוּמְשֵׁי תוֹרָה, אַרְבַּע אִמָּהוֹת, שְׁלֹשָׁה אָבוֹת, שְׁנֵי לֻחוֹת הַבְּרִית, אֶחָד אֱלֹהֵינוּ שֶׁבַּשָּׁמַיִם וּבָאָרֶץ.

עֲשָׂרָה מִי יוֹדֵעַ? עֲשָׂרָה אֲנִי יוֹדֵעַ: עֲשָׂרָה דִבְּרַיָּא, תִּשְׁעָה יַרְחֵי לֵדָה, שְׁמוֹנָה יְמֵי מִילָה, שִׁבְעָה יְמֵי שַׁבַּתָּא, שִׁשָּׁה סִדְרֵי מִשְׁנָה, חֲמִשָּׁה חוּמְשֵׁי תוֹרָה, אַרְבַּע אִמָּהוֹת, שְׁלֹשָׁה אָבוֹת, שְׁנֵי לֻחוֹת הַבְּרִית, אֶחָד אֱלֹהֵינוּ שֶׁבַּשָּׁמַיִם וּבָאָרֶץ.

אַחַד עָשָׂר מִי יוֹדֵעַ? אַחַד עָשָׂר אֲנִי יוֹדֵעַ: אַחַד עָשָׂר כּוֹכְבַיָּא, עֲשָׂרָה דִבְּרַיָּא, תִּשְׁעָה יַרְחֵי לֵדָה, שְׁמוֹנָה יְמֵי מִילָה, שִׁבְעָה יְמֵי שַׁבַּתָּא, שִׁשָּׁה סִדְרֵי מִשְׁנָה, חֲמִשָּׁה חוּמְשֵׁי תוֹרָה, אַרְבַּע אִמָּהוֹת, שְׁלֹשָׁה אָבוֹת, שְׁנֵי לֻחוֹת הַבְּרִית, אֶחָד אֱלֹהֵינוּ שֶׁבַּשָּׁמַיִם וּבָאָרֶץ.

שְׁנֵים עָשָׂר מִי יוֹדֵעַ? שְׁנֵים עָשָׂר אֲנִי יוֹדֵעַ: שְׁנֵים עָשָׂר שִׁבְטַיָּא, אַחַד עָשָׂר כּוֹכְבַיָּא, עֲשָׂרָה דִבְּרַיָּא, תִּשְׁעָה יַרְחֵי לֵדָה, שְׁמוֹנָה יְמֵי מִילָה, שִׁבְעָה יְמֵי שַׁבַּתָּא, שִׁשָּׁה סִדְרֵי מִשְׁנָה, חֲמִשָּׁה חוּמְשֵׁי תוֹרָה, אַרְבַּע אִמָּהוֹת, שְׁלֹשָׁה אָבוֹת, שְׁנֵי לֻחוֹת הַבְּרִית, אֶחָד אֱלֹהֵינוּ שֶׁבַּשָּׁמַיִם וּבָאָרֶץ.

שְׁלֹשָׁה עָשָׂר מִי יוֹדֵעַ? שְׁלֹשָׁה עָשָׂר אֲנִי יוֹדֵעַ: שְׁלֹשָׁה עָשָׂר מִדַּיָּא, שְׁנֵים עָשָׂר שִׁבְטַיָּא, אַחַד עָשָׂר כּוֹכְבַיָּא, עֲשָׂרָה דִבְּרַיָּא, תִּשְׁעָה יַרְחֵי לֵדָה, שְׁמוֹנָה יְמֵי מִילָה, שִׁבְעָה יְמֵי שַׁבַּתָּא, שִׁשָּׁה סִדְרֵי מִשְׁנָה, חֲמִשָּׁה חוּמְשֵׁי תוֹרָה, אַרְבַּע אִמָּהוֹת, שְׁלֹשָׁה אָבוֹת, שְׁנֵי לֻחוֹת הַבְּרִית, אֶחָד אֱלֹהֵינוּ שֶׁבַּשָּׁמַיִם וּבָאָרֶץ.

Who knows nine? I know nine! Nine are the months of childbirth. Eight are the days for circumcision. Seven are the days of the week. Six are the orders of the Mishnah. Five are the books of the Torah. Four are the Matriarchs. Three are the Patriarchs. Two are the Tablets of the Covenant. One is our God in heaven and on earth.

Who knows ten? I know ten! Ten are the commandments. Nine are the months of childbirth. Eight are the days for circumcision. Seven are the days of the week. Six are the orders of the Mishnah. Five are the books of the Torah. Four are the Matriarchs. Three are the Patriarchs. Two are the Tablets of the Covenant. One is our God in heaven and on earth.

Who knows eleven? I know eleven! Eleven are the stars (in Joseph's dream). Ten are the commandments. Nine are the months of childbirth. Eight are the days for circumcision. Seven are the days of the week. Six are the orders of the Mishnah. Five are the books of the Torah. Four are the Matriarchs. Three are the Patriarchs. Two are the Tablets of the Covenant. One is our God in heaven and on earth.

Who knows twelve? I know twelve! Twelve are the tribes. Eleven are the stars (in Joseph's dream). Ten are the commandments. Nine are the months of childbirth. Eight are the days for circumcision. Seven are the days of the week. Six are the orders of the Mishnah. Five are the books of the Torah. Four are the Matriarchs. Three are the Patriarchs. Two are the Tablets of the Covenant. One is our God in heaven and on earth.

Who knows thirteen? I know thirteen! Thirteen are the attributes of God. Twelve are the tribes. Eleven are the stars (in Joseph's dream). Ten are the commandments. Nine are the months of childbirth. Eight are the days for circumcision. Seven are the days of the week. Six are the orders of the Mishnah. Five are the books of the Torah. Four are the Matriarchs. Three are the Patriarchs. Two are the Tablets of the Covenant. One is our God in heaven and on earth.

חַד גַּדְיָא, חַד גַּדְיָא דְזַבִּין אַבָּא בִּתְרֵי זוּזֵי, חַד גַּדְיָא, חַד גַּדְיָא.

וְאָתָא **שׁוּנְרָא**, וְאָכְלָה לְגַדְיָא, דְזַבִּין אַבָּא בִּתְרֵי זוּזֵי, חַד גַּדְיָא, חַד גַּדְיָא.

וְאָתָא **כַלְבָּא**, וְנָשַׁךְ לְשׁוּנְרָא, דְאָכְלָה לְגַדְיָא, דְזַבִּין אַבָּא בִּתְרֵי זוּזֵי, חַד גַּדְיָא, חַד גַּדְיָא.

וְאָתָא **חוּטְרָא**, וְהִכָּה לְכַלְבָּא, דְנָשַׁךְ לְשׁוּנְרָא, דְאָכְלָה לְגַדְיָא, דְזַבִּין אַבָּא בִּתְרֵי זוּזֵי, חַד גַּדְיָא, חַד גַּדְיָא.

וְאָתָא **נוּרָא**, וְשָׂרַף לְחוּטְרָא, דְהִכָּה לְכַלְבָּא, דְנָשַׁךְ לְשׁוּנְרָא, דְאָכְלָה לְגַדְיָא, דְזַבִּין אַבָּא בִּתְרֵי זוּזֵי, חַד גַּדְיָא, חַד גַּדְיָא.

וְאָתָא **מַיָּא**, וְכָבָה לְנוּרָא, דְשָׂרַף לְחוּטְרָא, דְהִכָּה לְכַלְבָּא, דְנָשַׁךְ לְשׁוּנְרָא, דְאָכְלָה לְגַדְיָא, דְזַבִּין אַבָּא בִּתְרֵי זוּזֵי, חַד גַּדְיָא, חַד גַּדְיָא.

וְאָתָא **תוֹרָא**, וְשָׁתָא לְמַיָּא, דְכָבָה לְנוּרָא, דְשָׂרַף לְחוּטְרָא, דְהִכָּה לְכַלְבָּא, דְנָשַׁךְ לְשׁוּנְרָא, דְאָכְלָה לְגַדְיָא, דְזַבִּין אַבָּא בִּתְרֵי זוּזֵי, חַד גַּדְיָא, חַד גַּדְיָא.

וְאָתָא **הַשּׁוֹחֵט**, וְשָׁחַט לְתוֹרָא, דְשָׁתָא לְמַיָּא, דְכָבָה לְנוּרָא, דְשָׂרַף לְחוּטְרָא,דְהִכָּה לְכַלְבָּא, דְנָשַׁךְ לְשׁוּנְרָא, דְאָכְלָה לְגַדְיָא, דְזַבִּין אַבָּא בִּתְרֵי זוּזֵי, חַד גַּדְיָא, חַד גַּדְיָא.

וְאָתָא **מַלְאַךְ הַמָּוֶת**, וְשָׁחַט לְשׁוֹחֵט, דְשָׁחַט לְתוֹרָא, דְשָׁתָא

One kid, one kid, that father bought for two zuzim. One kid, one kid.

Then came a ***cat*** that ate the kid that father bought for two zuzim. One kid, one kid.

Then came a ***dog*** that bit the cat that ate the kid that father bought for two zuzim. One kid, one kid.

Then came a ***stick*** that beat the dog that bit the cat that ate the kid that father bought for two zuzim. One kid, one kid.

Then came a ***fire*** that burnt the stick that beat the dog that bit the cat that ate the kid that father bought for two zuzim. One kid, one kid.

Then ***water*** came and extinguished the fire that burnt the stick that beat the dog that bit the cat that ate the kid that father bought for two zuzim. One kid, one kid.

Then came an ***ox*** and drank the water that extinguished the fire that burnt the stick that beat the dog that bit the cat that ate the kid that father bought for two zuzim. One kid, one kid.

Then came ***the slaughterer*** and slaughtered the ox that drank the water that extinguished the fire that burnt the stick that beat the dog that bit the cat that ate the kid that father bought for two zuzim. One kid, one kid.

Then came the ***Angel of Death*** and slew the slaughterer who

לְמַיָּא, דְּכָבָה לְנוּרָא, דְּשָׂרַף לְחוּטְרָא, דְּהִכָּה לְכַלְבָּא, דְּנָשַׁךְ לְשׁוּנְרָא, דְּאָכְלָה לְגַדְיָא, דְּזַבִּין אַבָּא בִּתְרֵי זוּזֵי, חַד גַּדְיָא, חַד גַּדְיָא.

וְאָתָא הַקָּדוֹשׁ בָּרוּךְ הוּא, וְשָׁחַט לְמַלְאַךְ הַמָּוֶת, דְּשָׁחַט לְתוֹרָא, דְּשָׁתָא לְמַיָּא, דְּכָבָה לְנוּרָא, דְּשָׂרַף לְחוּטְרָא, דְּהִכָּה לְכַלְבָּא, דְּנָשַׁךְ לְשׁוּנְרָא, דְּאָכְלָה לְגַדְיָא, דְּזַבִּין אַבָּא בִּתְרֵי זוּזֵי, חַד גַּדְיָא, חַד גַּדְיָא.

♦ פירוש ♦

חַד גַּדְיָא

R' Nachman of Breslov explains that חד גדיה details the continuing struggle for control of this world—the war between holiness and evil.

The cat represents Yaakov's sons who were jealous of their brother (the kid) whom they sold into slavery. Because of this, they endured the Egyptian exile (the dog). Moshe's staff, represented by the stick, was used to strike the Egyptian. However, when the Golden Calf was made (the fire) holiness was once again subdued. We then received the Torah (the water). Once more holiness was elevated. However, this struggle between holiness and evil has endured. Eisav and his descendants (represented by the ox) challenge us in our present exile. Eventually, Moshiach ben Yosef (represented by the *shochet*) will subdue Eisav. Then the *malach hamoves*—the Angel of Death—will come and kill this Moshiach, as we learn in Succah 52. "At the end of days Hashem Himself will measure out the ultimate true justice." Once the *malach hamoves* is slaughtered, the world will be completely rectified.

♦ ♦ ♦ ♦ ♦ ♦

R' Avrohom Mordechai Alter, the third Gerrer Rebbe, said that the kid represents the Jewish nation. The kid was persecuted; there was a dog,

slaughtered the ox that drank the water that extinguished the fire that burnt the stick that beat the dog that bit the cat that ate the kid that father bought for two zuzim. One kid, one kid.

Then came ***the Holy One, Blessed be He,*** and killed the Angel of Death, who slew the slaughterer who slaughtered the ox that drank the water that extinguished the fire that burnt the stick that beat the dog that bit the cat that ate the kid that father bought for two zuzim. One kid, one kid.

♦ פירוש ♦

and then a fire. The events in this kabbalistic song could have been interpreted as happenstance. But one who studies the entire picture sees that from beginning to end there was a guiding hand.

So too, one who looks at Jewish history may see only a puzzling trail of persecution and destruction. When Moshiach comes, we will clearly see a pattern—and a purpose—in the seemingly unrelated persecutions. The pieces of the puzzle will fall into place, and we will see that there was, indeed, a master plan, orchestrated by the Master of the world.

♦ ♦ ♦ ♦ ♦ ♦

לשנה הבאה בירושלים!

Other seforim
by Rabbi Dovid Goldwasser:

Living on the Edge

Starving to Live

Elul

Something to Say

It Happened in Heaven

בת קול יוצאת

About the Author

Often recognized as the familiar, soothing voice heard daily on morning radio 91.1 FM WFMU and 1430 AM WNSW, Rabbi Dovid Goldwasser disseminates Torah to tens of thou sands on radio and through his many speaking engagements. He has galvanized audiences from every background with his eloquence and dynamism in his multiple roles of educator, author, *Jewish Press* columnist, community leader, noted lec turer and spiritual mentor of Congregation Bais Yitzchok in Brooklyn, New York.

Rabbi Goldwasser has also established a strong following as an author. *It Happened In Heaven*, a best seller, has been translated into many languages, including Hebrew, Serbian and Croatian. *Something to Say* features Rabbi Goldwasser's insights into the weekly Torah portion. *Starving to Live* addresses the problem of eating disorders from a Torah perspective. His most recent best-seller, *Living on the Edge*, recounts real-life stories of people in desperate circumstances.

As a veteran and expert in education, Rabbi Goldwasser is consulted regularly. His keen insight, as well as his caring and concern, have enabled him to offer guidance and support to countless individuals, couples and families who have sought his counsel.

Rabbi Goldwasser travels extensively throughout the world, speaking both in synagogues and in Jewish community cen ters. During the past few years he has made several trips to the war-torn communities in Bosnia, Serbia and Croatia. There, Rabbi Goldwasser offered encouragement and inspiration to those who suffered through the war and are now trying to rebuild their lives.

MW01520776